T0301936

An Analysis of

Marcel Mauss's

The Gift
The Form and Reason for
Exchange in Archaic Societies

Elizabeth Whitaker

Routledge
Taylor & Francis Group

LONDON AND NEW YORK

Published by Macat International Ltd
24:13 Coda Centre, 189 Munster Road, London SW6 6AW.

Distributed exclusively by Routledge
2 Park Square, Milton Park, Abingdon, Oxon OX14 4RN
605 Third Avenue, New York, NY 10017

Routledge is an imprint of the Taylor & Francis Group, an informa business

www.macat.com
info@macat.com

Cataloguing in Publication Data
A catalogue record for this book is available from the British Library.
Library of Congress Cataloguing-in-Publication Data is available upon request.
Cover illustration: Etienne Gilfillan

ISBN 978-1-912302-12-3 (hardback)
ISBN 978-1-912128-58-7 (paperback)
ISBN 978-1-912281-00-8 (e-book)

CONTENTS

THE MACAT LIBRARY

The Macat Library is a series of unique academic explorations of seminal works in the humanities and social sciences – books and papers that have had a significant and widely recognised impact on their disciplines. It has been created to serve as much more than just a summary of what lies between the covers of a great book. It illuminates and explores the influences on, ideas of, and impact of that book. Our goal is to offer a learning resource that encourages critical thinking and fosters a better, deeper understanding of important ideas.

Each publication is divided into three Sections: Influences, Ideas, and Impact. Each Section has four Modules. These explore every important facet of the work, and the responses to it.

This Section-Module structure makes a Macat Library book easy to use, but it has another important feature. Because each Macat book is written to the same format, it is possible (and encouraged!) to cross-reference multiple Macat books along the same lines of inquiry or research. This allows the reader to open up interesting interdisciplinary pathways.

To further aid your reading, lists of glossary terms and people mentioned are included at the end of this book (these are indicated by an asterisk [*] throughout) – as well as a list of works cited.

Macat has worked with the University of Cambridge to identify the elements of critical thinking and understand the ways in which six different skills combine to enable effective thinking.
Three allow us to fully understand a problem; three more give us the tools to solve it. Together, these six skills make up the **PACIER** model of critical thinking. They are:

ANALYSIS – understanding how an argument is built
EVALUATION – exploring the strengths and weaknesses of an argument
INTERPRETATION – understanding issues of meaning

CREATIVE THINKING – coming up with new ideas and fresh connections
PROBLEM-SOLVING – producing strong solutions
REASONING – creating strong arguments

To find out more, visit **WWW.MACAT.COM.**

CRITICAL THINKING AND *THE GIFT*

Primary critical thinking skill: ANALYSIS
Secondary critical thinking skill: INTERPRETATION

Marcel Mauss's 1925 essay *The Gift* is an enduring classic of sociological and anthropological analysis by a thinker who is one of the founding fathers of modern anthropology.

The Gift exploits Mauss's high-level analytical and interpretative skills to produce a brilliant investigation of the forms, meanings, and structures of gift-giving across a range of societies. Mauss, along with many others, had noted that in a wide range of societies – especially those without monetary exchange or legal structures – gift-giving and receiving was carried out according to strict customs and unwritten laws. What he sought to do in *The Gift* was to analyse the structures that governed how and when gifts were given, received, and reciprocated in order to grasp what implicit and unspoken reasons governed these structures. He also wanted to apply his interpretative skills to asking what such exchanges meant, in order to explore the implications his analysis might have for modern, western cultures. In Mauss's investigations, it became clear that gift-giving is, in many cultures, a crucial structural force, binding people together in a web of reciprocal commitments generated by the laws of gifting. Indeed, he concluded, gifts can be seen as the 'glue' of society.

ABOUT THE AUTHOR OF THE ORIGINAL WORK

Born in 1872, **Marcel Mauss** was a French sociologist best known for his studies of social behavior. After graduating in philosophy and law, he began working with Émile Durkheim, the 'father of French sociology,' who also happened to be Mauss's uncle. His influential short book *The Gift* was first published in the 1923–24 edition of the annual journal *L'Année Sociologique*, founded by Durkheim in 1898.

A committed socialist and political activist, Mauss shared many of his views in writing for—and also editing—political journals. He spoke out on a number of subjects, including prejudice against Jews and the abuse of political power. He died in Paris at the age of 77 in 1950.

ABOUT THE AUTHOR OF THE ANALYSIS

Dr Elizabeth Whitaker holds a PhD in anthropology from Emory University. She has taught at several American universities and is currently a senior lecturer at the Università degli Studi di Bologna, Italy. In addition to a forthcoming book on anthropology for a general audience, she is the author of *Measuring Mamma's Milk: Fascism and the Medicalization of Maternity in Italy* (Ann Arbor: University of Michigan Press, 2000).

ABOUT MACAT

GREAT WORKS FOR CRITICAL THINKING

Macat is focused on making the ideas of the world's great thinkers accessible and comprehensible to everybody, everywhere, in ways that promote the development of enhanced critical thinking skills.

It works with leading academics from the world's top universities to produce new analyses that focus on the ideas and the impact of the most influential works ever written across a wide variety of academic disciplines. Each of the works that sit at the heart of its growing library is an enduring example of great thinking. But by setting them in context – and looking at the influences that shaped their authors, as well as the responses they provoked – Macat encourages readers to look at these classics and game-changers with fresh eyes. Readers learn to think, engage and challenge their ideas, rather than simply accepting them.

'Macat offers an amazing first-of-its-kind tool for interdisciplinary learning and research. Its focus on works that transformed their disciplines and its rigorous approach, drawing on the world's leading experts and educational institutions, opens up a world-class education to anyone.'

Andreas Schleicher
Director for Education and Skills, Organisation for Economic
Co-operation and Development

'Macat is taking on some of the major challenges in university education ... They have drawn together a strong team of active academics who are producing teaching materials that are novel in the breadth of their approach.'

Prof Lord Broers,
former Vice-Chancellor of the University of Cambridge

'The Macat vision is exceptionally exciting. It focuses upon new modes of learning which analyse and explain seminal texts which have profoundly influenced world thinking and so social and economic development. It promotes the kind of critical thinking which is essential for any society and economy. This is the learning of the future.'

Rt Hon Charles Clarke, former UK Secretary of State for Education

'The Macat analyses provide immediate access to the critical conversation surrounding the books that have shaped their respective discipline, which will make them an invaluable resource to all of those, students and teachers, working in the field.'

Professor William Tronzo, University of California at San Diego

WAYS IN TO THE TEXT

KEY POINTS

- Marcel Mauss (1872–1950) was a French sociologist known for his contributions to the study of social behavior, his academic collaborations, and his political activism.

- *The Gift* showed that reciprocal* exchanges (the simultaneous exchange of gifts) are expressions of social relationships that bind individuals and groups through obligations that extend forward in time.

- The book is distinctive for the range of ethnographic* material described (that is, the depth of its study in terms of peoples and cultures), the significance of its findings, and the relevance of the analysis to social science, politics, and personal life.

Who Was Marcel Mauss?

Marcel Mauss, the author of *The Gift* (1923–4), was born in 1872 in Épinal, northeastern France. After leaving university he became an important figure in French academic sociology* (the study of social behavior) and remained so for 50 years. Mauss spent most of his life working on research projects, often in collaboration with other scholars, and editing professional journals. He was very active politically, too, joining the cooperative movement* (backing the idea that businesses should be owned by the people who work for them) and writing for socialist* publications; the general principles of socialism are that everyone has some share in the distribution of power and money. Mauss spoke out against anti-Semitism*—prejudice against Jewish people—and the abuse of political power. He spoke many languages and read ancient Greek, Latin, and Sanskrit.

After studying philosophy and law, Mauss worked closely with his uncle, Émile Durkheim,* an influential figure known as the "father of French sociology"; the two shared an interest in working out how people think by analyzing their cultural* beliefs, legal systems, and social institutions.*

On Durkheim's death in 1917, Mauss took over the journal that Durkheim had founded 20 years earlier, *L'Année Sociologique.** His book *The Gift*, discussing the relationship between his uncle's sociological theories, ancient laws, and recent data collected by anthropologists* (those who study humans, past and present, around the world), first appeared in the 1923–4 issue of this journal. The piece highlights the differences between one-off and ongoing exchanges between people, and offers a consideration of the relationship between economic activity, social behavior, belief systems, and notions of morality.

What Does *The Gift* Say?

Mauss's book *The Gift: The Form and Reason for Exchange in Archaic Societies* argues that people do not give things without expecting something back in return, either consciously or subconsciously. The analysis looks at the giving and receiving of objects, people, and intangible goods in archaic societies* (Mauss uses the term "archaic" to designate indigenous and ancient societies that operate without money but not without trade* and bartering*). Everyday economic transactions and larger cycles of gifts and return-gifts coexist in all societies; Mauss focuses on reciprocal transfers because they tie together individuals and groups in long-term relationships. His study focuses on societies in which everything from property to titles "is there for passing on, and for balancing accounts."[1]

Mauss highlights the intertwining of economic systems with social systems, politics, and morality. His analysis shows how precise laws and customs regulate exchanges in small, face-to-face societies and identifies similar patterns in earlier gift systems that have survived in industrialized societies. He concludes with the observation that looking at economic exchange from an anthropological point of view could influence public policy, and suggests that a fairer politico-economic system might come out of analyzing and expanding institutionalized forms of reciprocity—the principle of mutual exchange.

The Gift is an extremely detailed work in which Mauss analyzes each society's gift exchange rules within its own specific social, historical, and cultural context, reflecting his firmly held belief that all aspects of society deserve equal consideration—that is, that the study of material and technological factors is just as important as the study of religious and moral beliefs. *The Gift* shows how social systems and cultural beliefs help shape and give meaning to human behavior. These ideas also run through Mauss's other work on religion, seasonality* (changes in a society's activities according to season), and personhood* (the idea of being an individual).

One of the few texts that he wrote without a coauthor, *The Gift* is Mauss's most famous work. One of the ways his ideas spread was through a mutual exchange of ideas with work colleagues; in turn, those ideas spread through further exchanges with other people. But the case could be made that, had he been less of a collaborative scholar, he might have found more influence. Assessing Mauss's impact, two scholars of anthropological history note that he is "less well known than he might have been had his work appeared in a more compact form—it is scattered widely, most of it is short, and much of it is in collaboration, so that the value of his truly unusual contribution is hard to assess, although present-day social science is shot through with the results of his thinking."[2]

Mauss's short book has had an enormous impact on both academia and literature. The book has been translated into English three times, most recently in 2015. It continues to inspire intellectual activity throughout the humanities (fields such as languages, literature, and philosophy) and the social sciences (fields such as history, economics, and political science), and remains a pivotal text in sociology and anthropology.

Why Does *The Gift* Matter?

The Gift is useful for analyzing economic behavior in any setting. It provides insights into what motivates people and the meaning of economic concepts such as rationality* (in economics, a characteristic of reasoning in which costs and benefits are weighed so that the best decision might be made) and utility* (the usefulness of anything paid for). The book explores how economics and social and cultural systems affect each other. It is also relevant to studies of legal codes and political philosophy. The analysis provides a guide for understanding common themes across different sets of data. The last part of the book illustrates how events influence intellectual ideas. Mauss struggled to make sense of the political turmoil in Europe after World War I. His conclusions for Western society remain controversial and are relevant to the ethical concerns of the time.

The Gift provides food for thought on the meaning of gift-giving across cultures and the presumed lack of meaning of financial transactions beyond the purely functional. The book sheds light on the contradictory mixture of values that are part of giving, receiving, and giving in return. In reciprocal exchange, generosity and selflessness meet self-interest and binding obligation.

The book expands on gift-giving in our own society and any assumptions of purely unselfish motives, showing that it involves the values and expectations Mauss identifies in simpler societies. In personal life and in the workplace, transfers of favors and resources demand a return. They solidify relationships and bring both honor and status.

At the same time, the book shows that commercial transactions are not altogether disconnected from human relationships. Money itself is a cultural product supported by a specific social and legal framework. The book explains why money alone cannot compensate the giving that goes into paid labor—given the talent, creative energy, wisdom, knowledge, and so on that the laborer invests in his or her work. Likewise, financial measures alone do not capture many kinds of job performance. The book sheds light on what people's spending behavior achieves and says about them. *The Gift* calls into question the assumption that individuals act and think in isolation.

The Gift is a book for all disciplines. It is a thorough analysis of a single topic that is also relevant to universal themes of existence. Whether in the lives of individuals or as the focus of intellectual analysis, reciprocal gift exchange is a human activity fraught with ambiguity. The book's staying power is a testament to our timeless fascination with social interaction.

NOTES

1 Marcel Mauss, *The Gift: The Form and Reason for Exchange in Archaic Societies* (London: Routledge, 1990), 14.

2 Paul Bohanan and Mark Glazer (eds), *High Points in Anthropology* (New York: Alfred A. Knopf, 1988), 264.

SECTION 1
INFLUENCES

MODULE 1
THE AUTHOR AND THE
HISTORICAL CONTEXT

KEY POINTS

- Marcel Mauss's *The Gift* has had a lasting effect on the way anthropologists* and other scholars approach the analysis of cultures* in which economics, politics, technology, and individual motivations are intertwined.

- Mauss's academic training in sociology* (the study of social behavior, social institutions, and the origins and organization of human society), law, religion, and languages uniquely prepared him for comparative analyses* of cultural systems including gift exchange. In comparative analysis, research is conducted by a comparison of different systems, artifacts, or features.

- The political turmoil of the early twentieth century set the stage for Mauss's approach to ethnographic* material (information derived from the study of a group of people in the field—that is, in their own setting) and its implications for industrialized societies.

Why Read This Text?

Marcel Mauss's *The Gift: The Form and Reason for Exchange in Archaic Societies* concerns a topic close to everyone's heart: social relationships.[1] A second question is the degree to which individuals determine their own thoughts and actions as opposed to being controlled by society and culture. The book addresses both questions and contributes to scholarly knowledge about humans as members of groups.

Mauss explores the ways in which gifts and return gifts join people in cycles of exchange that are governed by rules and infused with

> ❝ Where anthropology is concerned he [Mauss] would surely be more than satisfied. Nothing has been the same since. The big developments stem from this work. ❞
>
> Mary Douglas,* "Foreword: No Free Gifts" in *The Gift*

cultural values. He provides a unifying interpretation of cross-cultural data and advances the sociological approach developed by his uncle, the pioneering sociologist Émile Durkheim.* Mauss's short book opens a window on the history of ideas, shares a wealth of fascinating ethnographic detail, and outlines a method for comparative analysis. The book provides food for thought on the connection between reciprocal* exchange (roughly, a system of mutual exchanges) and social cohesion—the stability enjoyed by a functioning society. Mauss reflects on what the study of small, face-to-face societies suggests about how to alter economic systems in industrialized societies for the common good.

In contrast to earlier scholars, Mauss showed that economic, political, religious, kinship* (the way in which a people formally recognizes relationships of different kinds), and other systems do not exist apart from one another. In line with Durkheim's thinking he focused on the shared ideas and institutionalized rules and procedures that form the context for individual beliefs and behaviors. Mauss did not foreground any single factor such as ecological forces or material constraints as the main force behind sociocultural systems. And although he accepted the idea that societies evolve and become more complicated, he made it very clear that complex societies were not necessarily better than simpler societies.

Mauss communicated his and Durkheim's ideas to colleagues and younger contemporaries such as the influential French anthropologist Claude Lévi-Strauss,* as well as students including the psychoanalyst and anthropologist Georges Devereux,* the pioneering anthropologist of Africa Denise Paulme,* and the filmmaker and anthropologist Jean Rouch.* Through them, Mauss's influence reached the thinkers Pierre Bourdieu,* Georges Condominas,* and many others.[2]

Author's Life

Marcel Mauss was born in 1872 in Épinal, in the Lorraine region of northeastern France, to parents who both worked in textile businesses. Although his family was Orthodox Jewish, Mauss was not a religious man. His relatives included many scholars, most notably his maternal uncle, Émile Durkheim, who is considered the father of sociology. Mauss's much-younger cousin and Durkheim's niece, the marine biologist Claudette Raphael Bloch, was the mother of the British anthropologist Maurice Bloch* (born 1939).

After his university education in Bordeaux, where his uncle held France's first professorship in sociology and education, Mauss moved to Paris in 1895 to continue his studies. He spent two years (1897–8) traveling in England and the Netherlands before returning to Paris where he started lecturing in 1900, first at the École Pratique des Hautes Études, and after 1930 at the Collège de France.

Mauss actively engaged with the political upheavals that troubled Europe throughout his adult life. He joined the collectivist* student movement, the French Workers' Party,* and the Revolutionary Socialist Workers' Party,* all left-wing movements, and wrote for leftist publications including *La Vie Socialiste, Humanité,* and *Le Mouvement Socialiste.* Mauss wrote in support of the novelist and playwright Émile Zola,* whose public criticism of the French military for its anti-Semitism* (anti-Jewish sentiment) and military interference with legal procedure in the trial of Alfred Dreyfus* led to Dreyfus being cleared of the accusations made against him. Mauss continued to speak out against anti-Semitism and racism throughout his life, and his consciousness of political questions and dimensions are evident throughout his work, including in *The Gift.*[3]

Durkheim's death in 1917 was followed by a backlash against the curricular changes he had helped institute throughout France as a professor of pedagogy (the method and practice of teaching). Mauss, an advocate of Durkheim's sociological approach, retreated into administrative activity. He took over direction of the journal *L'Année Sociologique*,* which had been founded by Durkheim in 1898 and had lost many of its main contributors to World War I* (1914–18), including the sociologists Henri Beauchat* and Robert Hertz.* In 1925–6, Mauss cofounded the Institut d'Ethnologie* at the University of Paris with the ethnographer Paul Rivet* and the sociologist Lucien Lévy-Bruhl.* Mauss co-directed and lectured at the Institut until 1939. World War II* (1939–45) brought Mauss further losses and grief, which, combined with personal and domestic troubles, led him to cease his scholarly work. He died in Paris in 1950.[4]

Author's Background

Marcel Mauss was a broadly trained scholar who learned many languages including Russian, Greek, Sanskrit, Latin, and Malayo-Polynesian. At the University of Bordeaux he studied philosophy and law. After coming in third place in the civil service examination in 1895, Mauss chose to pursue further education at the École Pratique des Hautes Études in Paris, one of France's publicly funded selective academic and research institutes. Mauss studied comparative religion and ancient Greek, Roman, Indian, and Germanic literature and philosophy. Between 1897 and 1898 he traveled to the Netherlands and England, where he worked briefly with Edward Burnett Tylor,* the first university professor of anthropology in Britain. Tylor's holistic* definition of culture—a definition of culture concerned with the interdependence of its components—continues to be cited today, though with important caveats about variability and change.[5]

From 1902 to 1930, Mauss taught a course on "L'histoire des religions des peuples non-civilisés" ("The History of the Religions of

Non-Civilized Peoples") at the École Pratique des Hautes Études. From 1930 to 1939 he offered the same course at the Collège de France, another of France's prestigious seats of learning.[6] His enduring interest in comparative religion contributed to his work on gift exchange as a social phenomenon.

During the early interwar years, Mauss continued to explore political philosophy as a socialist* and member of the cooperative movement* in France (a movement in which workers coowned the companies they worked for). Looking to communist* Russia, however, he was deeply disturbed by the government's destruction of cooperatives, its authoritarianism (the authority it demanded over the lives of its citizens), and rejection of the principles of the market economy* (that is, principles of economic exchange of goods based on established calculated values).[7] In *The Gift*, Mauss defends individualism as a motivator of productive activity and social participation, but points out the exploitation that is possible where transactions are construed as separate from their moral and social context.

NOTES

1   Marcel Mauss, *The Gift: The Form and Reason for Exchange in Archaic Societies* (London: Routledge, 1990).

2   Mary Douglas, "Foreword: No Free Gifts," in *The Gift* by Marcel Mauss (London: Routledge, 2000); Walter Goldschmidt, "Untitled Review of *The Gift* by Marcel Mauss," *American Anthropologist* 57, no. 6 (1955): 1299–1300; Seth Leacock, "The Ethnological Theory of Marcel Mauss," *American Anthropologist* 56 (1954): 58–71.

3   Marcel Fournier, *Marcel Mauss: A Biography* (Princeton, NJ: Princeton University Press, 2005), 4.

4   Paul Bohannan and Mark Glazer (eds), *High Points in Anthropology* (New York: Alfred A. Knopf, 1988), 264–6; Goldschmidt, "Untitled Review," 1299; Leacock, "The Ethnological Theory," 58–9, 64–5.

5 "Culture or Civilization, taken in its wide ethnographic sense, is that complex whole which includes knowledge, belief, art, morals, law, custom, and any other capabilities and habits acquired by man as a member of society." Edward Burnett Tylor, *Primitive Culture*: *Researches into the Development of Mythology, Philosophy, Religion, Art, and Custom* (London: J. Murray, 1871), 1.

6 Upon succeeding Mauss at the École Pratique des Hautes Études, Lévi-Strauss renamed the course "Comparative Religion of Non-Literate Peoples."

7 Leacock, "The Ethnological Theory," 58–61, 64–5; Bohannan and Glazer, *High Points*, 264–6.

MODULE 2
ACADEMIC CONTEXT

KEY POINTS

- Anthropology* is the study of the biological and cultural history and current variability of humankind. *The Gift* is a comparative study of gift exchange as a central institution*—in the sense of a conventionalized activity— that structures relationships and channels the flow of goods, people, and intangibles such as rituals and titles.

- In the early twentieth century, sociologists* (scholars of the history and structure of society) and anthropologists sought both to document the features of non-Western societies and to classify and make sense of the information in terms of social evolutionary* stages (according to social evolutionary principles, societies progress through a fixed series of stages of ever-increasing technological, social, and intellectual perfection).

- Marcel Mauss collaborated with scholars including the sociologists Paul Fauconnet* and Émile Durkheim* seeking to identify overarching patterns to cultural institutions.

The Work in its Context

At the time of Marcel Mauss's writing of *The Gift*, French sociology was dominated by the work of Mauss's uncle, Émile Durkheim. The backdrop for Durkheim's sociology, in turn, was French philosophy's turn-of-the-century rejection of English utilitarianism*—a philosophical and liberal* political tradition that presumed individual rationality* was the elemental, positive force driving modern economic life.[1] French philosophers argued that radical individualism failed to account for the social context of individual actions and beliefs.

> ❝ In the economic and legal systems that have preceded
> our own, one hardly ever finds a simple exchange of
> goods, wealth, and products in transactions concluded
> by individuals. First, it is not individuals but collectivities
> that impose obligations of exchange and contract upon
> each other ... Moreover, what they exchange is not
> solely property and wealth, movable and immovable
> goods, and things economically useful. In particular,
> such exchanges are acts of politeness ... Finally, these
> total services and counter-services are committed to in a
> somewhat voluntary form by presents and gifts, although
> in the final analysis they are strictly compulsory, on pain
> of private or public warfare. ❞
>
> Marcel Mauss, *The Gift: The Form and Reason for Exchange in Archaic Societies*

That is, the British view ignored the relationship between economic and social organization, and overlooked how cultural beliefs and social position could affect the choices an individual makes. French philosophers including Alexis de Tocqueville* argued that radical individualism led to exploitation and resulted in people being alienated from society and disengaged from politics.

Durkheim proposed a middle ground between thinking of an individual as separate from society and seeing him or her as being completely controlled by social context. Although critics have often concluded that the individual was unimportant to his sociological science, Durkheim was intensely interested in the degree to which the political and social systems of different types of society allowed individual personhood* to flourish. Durkheim focused on identifying shared norms and rules and assessing their effect on individual choice. He did not dismiss the force of individual will, but as a sociologist his task was to explain social dynamics and identify collective representations* (shared beliefs and understandings). Together with Paul Fauconnet, Mauss laid out Durkheim's theoretical approach in a 1901 article for the French encyclopedia *La Grande Encyclopédie*.[2]

Although he worked with material from small, non-Western societies, Mauss considered himself a sociologist. French sociology continued to encompass anthropology long after the latter became a separate science elsewhere.[3] In the United Kingdom and United States, anthropology was concerned with the comparative study of all societies and especially non-Western ones, whereas sociology tended to focus on the internal workings of industrialized societies.

Overview of the Field

Durkheim's 1897 book *On Suicide*, for which Mauss compiled the data, illustrated the effect of social forces on individual behavior.[4] Durkheim's analysis of the variability in suicide rates across social groups, nations, and time showed that mental distress did just not occur randomly as a result of biological or chance factors. The study illustrated his trademark analytical approach, shared by Mauss: empirical,* objective, detailed examination of working systems in all their complexity ("empirical" study is research founded on evidence verifiable by observation). Durkheim and Mauss were ahead of their time in recognizing that their own inherited collective representations and politico-economic systems affected their interpretation of other cultures.*

Their caution is evident in Mauss's uncertainty about social evolution. He taught that all societies were civilized, albeit in different ways.[5] This was a clear departure from the progressive logic of nineteenth- and early twentieth-century explorers, missionaries, and theorists such as the British philosopher Herbert Spencer* and the US anthropologist Lewis Henry Morgan,* who believed societies could be ranked like animal species into forms of ever-increasing complexity and perfection.[6] To illustrate, while remarking on the similarities in gift exchange across societies widely dispersed around the Pacific Ocean, Mauss notes the presence of comparable systems in Africa, Asia, and the Americas. In *The Gift*, he refuses to engage in the ongoing debate about whether similar customs in different societies are the result of diffusion or independent invention.[7]

Mauss does, however, concentrate his study on existing archaic societies* similarly placed on an evolutionary scale. He also looks at societies that came before modern Indo-European societies and searches for "survivals" in present-day customs (that is, features that have endured from ancient social practices). Looking backward, he proposes a model for how the primordial societies managed economic exchanges. Yet throughout the three-stage progression Mauss finds that the same basic principles apply, and therefore that no society is superior to another.

Academic Influences

At the time of Mauss's writing, anthropology had moved from the study to the field. *The Gift* was made possible by the on-the-ground work of anthropologists such as Bronislaw Malinowski* in the Pacific Trobriand Islands and Franz Boas* along the Northwest Coast of North America. Mauss's approach to the material was the product of many influences. At Bordeaux, these included the philosophers Alfred Victor Espinas,* who studied the collective genius behind technological and cultural traditions and forms, and the philosopher Octave Hamelin,* who was interested in the binding effect of human relationships.[8] Mauss collaborated on research with Durkheim and other members of the original group of contributors to the influential journal *L'Année Sociologique.**

While Mauss shared the prevailing view that it was useful to examine simpler or more "primitive" forms of social facts because they show the basic features of the later ones, he did not agree with people—including Morgan—who said civilizations always progressed onward and upward, from barbarism to savagery to civilization.[9] Likewise, Mauss's course on comparative religion at the École Pratique des Hautes Études departed from the standard teachings encapsulated by the Scottish anthropologist James Frazer's* 12-volume *The Golden Bough*.[10] Frazer believed that human thought progressed from primitive magic to religion and finally to science, abandoning the logic of affinity* (the principle of "like attracts like") and contagion* (the principle in "primitive" magic that mystical forces are present in things such as body products, and can be manipulated for magical purposes) for true understanding of cause and effect. Mauss rejected Frazer's framework along with his method of ethnological* comparison (the comparison of material produced by the systematic study of a particular people) in which he used snippets of material out of context and combined them to suit his aims.[11]

Mauss's approach was methodical and evidence-based. Like Boas, he resisted deductive (or top-down) theories about the impact of evolutionary, psychological, geographical, racial, or economic forces on social systems and individual behavior.[12] Mauss preferred Durkheim's method of searching within and across cases for social systems, politico-legal institutions, and shared beliefs that set the parameters for action without simply dictating it.

NOTES

1   Mary Douglas, "Foreword: No Free Gifts," in *The Gift* by Marcel Mauss (London: Routledge, 2000).

2   Paul Fauconnet and Marcel Mauss, "Sociologie: Objet et Méthode," *La Grande Encyclopédie* 30 (1901): 165–76.

3   Seth Leacock, "The Ethnological Theory of Marcel Mauss," *American Anthropologist* 56 (1954): 60.

4   Émile Durkheim, *On Suicide* (London: Penguin Books, 2006).

5   Leacock, "The Ethnological Theory," 60.

6   Lewis Henry Morgan, *Ancient Society: Researches into the Lines of Human Progress from Savagery through Barbarism to Civilization* (New York: Henry Holt, 1877).

7   Marcel Mauss, *The Gift: The Form and Reason for Exchange in Archaic Societies* (London: Routledge, 1990), 97–8.

8   Paul Bohannan and Mark Glazer (eds), *High Points in Anthropology* (New York: Alfred A. Knopf, 1988), 264.

9   For instance, Morgan was so certain of the progression of societies from savagery to barbarism to civilization that he invented taxonomic categories without evidence. He assumed that sooner or later the requisite social customs or kinship systems would be found to fill in the gaps. Morgan, *Ancient Society*.

10   James George Frazer, *The Golden Bough* (New York: Simon and Schuster, 1996).

11   Marcel Mauss, "L'Enseignement de l'Histoire des Religions des Peuples Non-Civilisés à l'École des Hautes Études," *Revue de l'Histoire des Religions* 45 (1902): 36–55; Fredrik Barth et al., *One Discipline, Four Ways: British, German, French, and American Anthropology* (Chicago: University of Chicago Press, 2005); Leacock, "The Ethnological Theory," 61.

12   Franz Boas, *Race, Language, and Culture* (London: Collier-Macmillan, 1940).

MODULE 3
THE PROBLEM

KEY POINTS

- The overarching question that sociologists* sought to address at the time of Mauss's analysis of *The Gift* was how societies are organized and how their structure is related to the way they function.

- Some scholars assumed that societies evolved through a fixed series of technological, social, and intellectual advances; for others, social forms were determined by material, technological, or biological factors; others still concentrated on documenting languages, customs, and ways of life in all their historical and local particularity.

- Mauss focused on the exchange of property, persons, and services in societies believed to occupy the same social evolutionary level. He sought regularities across cases but considered each one in context, without speculating on ultimate causes.

Core Question

The core question that Marcel Mauss addresses in *The Gift* is: what is the purpose, meaning, and legal ordering of exchange in societies without money or laws governing contracts? Mauss found that ethnographers*— those engaged in the study of people and their culture—were often perplexed that people in archaic societies* (indigenous and similar, extinct, societies), followed precise rules about how gifts were to be offered, accepted, and repaid. What seemed to escape the outsiders' notice was that exchange involved time scales and interconnected moral and material transfers that, once mapped out, revealed the contours, hierarchies, dynamism, and cohesion of a given society.

> 66 The subject is clear. In Scandinavian civilization, and in a good number of others, exchanges and contracts take place in the form of presents; in theory these are voluntary, in reality they are given and reciprocated obligatorily. 99

Marcel Mauss, *The Gift: The Form and Reason for Exchange in Archaic Societies*

The topic of exchange was related to a question about individuality that interested Émile Durkheim.* Both Durkheim and Mauss believed that individual personhood* was relatively undeveloped in the simplest societies, in which the family or clan* (relatives sharing a common ancestor) was everything and solidarity*—connectedness—was "mechanical," or the automatic result of low specialization of tasks and roles. At the opposite extreme, in industrialized societies individual personhood was elevated to excess; social relations enveloped people but were not acknowledged. Here "organic" solidarity came about through the interdependence of specialized functions. Individuality, rather than belonging, was everything.[1]

While Durkheim assumed that individual personhood in societies between these extremes remained trapped beneath a dense net of social ties and cultural beliefs, Mauss showed that individuals are motivated to participate in gift exchange by a mixture of prestige and honor with material gain. They exercise self-interest. Moreover, interactions as a whole represent a system that is consistent and predictable, even in contexts without market* transactions (that is, in contexts where things are exchanged purely according to agreed values). In either case, exchange is connected to status, but while reciprocal* giving is public and observable and therefore more exacting about fairness, market exchange is hidden and consequently further removed from personal and group honor.

Mauss concludes that, fundamentally, we are all the same—it is just social context that makes us behave differently. So the differences are ones of degree, not kind, and he suggests that market societies should revive the mutually binding elements of economic exchange in the interests of individual and collective well-being.[2]

The Participants

Mauss spent his entire career collaborating closely with other scholars. His work reveals a trajectory of thought that is both shared and distinctive. The results are evident in *The Gift*.

Mauss's 1903 article coauthored with Durkheim, *Primitive Classification*, explores how simple societies categorize objects, people, and phenomena.[3] The authors propose a connection between logical categories and social divisions such as those between men and women or between clans and tribes* (a category in a society politically organized around kinship* relations and classes). In other words, conceptual and linguistic categories are not inherent in the nature of things but are, rather, socially constructed.

Mauss and Durkheim extended these ideas to a developing theory of the sacred*—the sphere of ideas, rituals, and objects considered worthy of religious veneration. Durkheim's 1912 book on comparative religion, *The Elementary Forms of the Religious Life,* explores how society symbolizes itself in "totems"*—inert objects conceptually transformed into sacred things with mystical power—with the result that social categories are mapped onto nature.[4] Mauss and the historian and sociologist Henri Hubert's* 1899 work on animal sacrifice in ancient India and early Judaism, "Essai sur la Nature et la Fonction du Sacrifice" ("Essay on the Nature and Function of Sacrifice"), identifies the concept of the *sacré* (sacred), which grants the sacrificial gift the power to demand a return gift from the gods.[5] Their 1904 publication on magic, *A General Theory of Magic*, focuses on the Polynesian* and Australo-Melanesian* concept of *mana*:*[6] the mobile spiritual force that pervades the universe, attaches to objects, and reveals itself through some people's advantages and powers.[7]

In a 1906 article on Eskimo* (Inuit) migrations written with the sociologist Henri Beauchat,* *Seasonal Variation of the Eskimo: A Study in Social Morphology*, Mauss shows that the customs governing winter convergence and summer dispersal of groups cannot be explained in simple ecological terms such as the availability of animals to hunt.[8] Mauss and Beauchat argue that the same principle applies to the seasonal variability in activity among other populations. The article contributes to a body of work that established the social origins of beliefs and practices that other scholars saw as the result of biological needs, universal mental constructs, or the physical laws of nature.

The Contemporary Debate

Mauss's analysis in *The Gift* is based on the work of scholars including Bronislaw Malinowski* in the Pacific Trobriand Islands, the British philosopher and anthropologist* A. R. Radcliffe-Brown* in the Andaman Islands and Western Australia, and the German American anthropologist Franz Boas* on the Northwest Coast of North America.[9] Each of these ethnographers had a profound impact on anthropology and sociology.

Radcliffe-Brown drew upon Durkheim's thoughts about collective representations and social institutions* in his development of British structural-functionalism.*[10] Structural-functionalism is based on an analogy between society and the human body. The will or actions of individual people—compared to cells in the analogy—do not fundamentally alter the system, at least not on their own. Malinowski, who with Radcliffe-Brown founded British social anthropology (the comparative analysis* of human societies), differed from this school of thought in giving more weight to the individual and in his belief that society is born out of basic human biological and psychological needs.[11]

Franz Boas took a different approach to ethnography known as historical particularism.* Boas avoided deductive theorizing in favor of thorough data collection and intensive study of indigenous* languages (the languages spoken by a place's first inhabitants).[12] Through the use of evidence verifiable by observation, Boas demonstrated change through examples such as kinship* systems (systems that define how people are related), art forms, and even head shape, and in the process challenged prevailing racial and evolutionary theories and the idea that societies tend to remain stable through automatic regulation of internal variables.[13]

Mauss's analysis of gift exchange combines elements from each of these perspectives. Mauss takes structural-functionalist premises for granted but also accounts for individual motivation. In line with Boas, he resists the idea that some societies or customs are superior to others and examines institutions in context, pays attention to change, and does not take a deterministic view of causation (that is, the idea that one or more variables directly produces a specific outcome). At the same time Mauss focuses on similarities between cultures in order to support general laws and sustain a loosely evolutionary progression from simpler to more complex societies.

NOTES

1   Émile Durkheim, *The Division of Labor in Society* (New York: Free Press, 1984).

2   Marcel Mauss, *The Gift: The Form and Reason for Exchange in Archaic Societies* (London: Routledge, 1990).

3   Émile Durkheim and Marcel Mauss, *Primitive Classification* (Chicago: University of Chicago Press, 1963).

4   Émile Durkheim, *The Elementary Forms of the Religious Life* (New York: Free Press, 1915).

5   Marcel Mauss and Henri Hubert, "Essai sur la Nature et la Fonction du Sacrifice," *L'Année Sociologique* (1897–98): 29–138.

6   Marcel Mauss and Henri Hubert, *A General Theory of Magic* (London: Routledge, 2001).

7   Durkheim, *The Elementary Forms,* 223.

8   Marcel Mauss and Henri Beauchat, *Seasonal Variation of the Eskimo: A Study in Social Morphology* (London: Routledge, 1979).

9   Malinowski's treatise on inter-island exchange relationships in the Trobriand Islands appeared three years before *The Gift*. In the same year, Radcliffe-Brown published the final analysis of fieldwork completed some 15 years before in the Andaman Islands; a decade earlier, he had published the results of fieldwork in Western Australia. Boas published articles and books on the populations of the Northwest Coast of North America from the late nineteenth century through 1940.

10 Alfred Reginald Radcliffe-Brown, *The Andaman Islanders* (Cambridge: Cambridge University Press, 1933).

11 Bronislaw Malinowski, *Argonauts of the Western Pacific: An Account of Native Enterprise and Adventure in the Archipelagos of Melanesian New Guinea* (London: Routledge, 1922).

12 Franz Boas, "The Limitations of the Comparative Method of Anthropology," *Science* 4, no. 103 (1896): 901–8; Franz Boas, "Changes in Bodily Form of Descendants of Immigrants," *American Anthropologist* 14, no. 3 (1912): 530–62.

13 See for example Boas's discussion of patrilineal and matrilineal kinship among tribes of the Northwest Coast of North America: Franz Boas, *Kwakiutl Ethnography* (Chicago: University of Chicago Press, 1966).

MODULE 4
THE AUTHOR'S CONTRIBUTION

KEY POINTS

- Mauss shows that societies without modern forms of currency* (a medium of exchange such as cash, or shells, say) nonetheless have legal, political, and economic systems that regulate the flow of goods and services.

- By explaining the moral and material aspects of exchange in face-to-face societies, Mauss identifies a common thread in diverse ethnographic* studies and provides a model for understanding human interaction in mass society.

- The analysis unites state-of-the art theoretical perspectives on social institutions* (codified relationships or activities) and collective representations* (shared beliefs and understandings) with contemporary methods of empirical* research and comparative analysis.* Comparative analysis requires the examination of two or more cases to identify similarities and differences that might explain their respective outcomes.

Author's Aims

Marcel Mauss's aim in *The Gift* is to explain the binding obligations created by gift exchange in simple societies. To this end, he combines ethnographic evidence gathered by other scholars with his own studies of ancient languages and philosophies. His analysis focuses on the shared features among norms governing exchange relationships across societies.

Mauss shows that simple societies have devised rules that structure the transfer of valuables of all kinds, tangible and intangible. The

66 The circulation of goods follows that of men, women, and children, of feasts, rituals, ceremonies, and dances, and even that of jokes and insults. All in all, it is one and the same. If one gives things and returns them, it is because one is giving and receiving 'respects'—we still say 'courtesies.' Yet, it is also because by giving one is giving *oneself*, and if one gives *oneself*, it is because one 'owes' *oneself*—one's person and one's goods—to others. 99

Marcel Mauss, *The Gift: The Form and Reason for Exchange in Archaic Societies*

institution of gift exchange is related to other social institutions such as marriage or religious practices and contributes to social solidarity* (support and connectedness) and stability. By identifying the legal, social, political, and moral aspects of economic exchange, Mauss sheds a new light on the concepts of utility* (in economics, the material or psychological usefulness of purchased goods to the purchaser) and rational* self-interest (the weighing of costs and benefits to arrive at a decision). Participation in gift cycles is at once voluntary and obligatory, rewarding and costly, material and spiritual. Mauss also shows that the economic exchange systems of simple and complex societies are not radically different but rather operate according to similar principles. Complex societies contain remnants of the more socially significant economic exchanges characteristic of simpler societies.

The structure of the book clearly reflects the author's aims and approach. Mauss begins by describing a basic system of generalized give-and-take or reciprocity* (the principle that acts or material gifts should be met with a return, often in a formalized or cyclical fashion) in small societies throughout the world. He then analyzes an extremely competitive form characterized by built-in escalation—that each gift be greater than the last, not just equivalent—and even the destruction of property as a display of status. Mauss demonstrates the survival of similar practices in the languages, laws, and customs of modern descendants of ancient civilizations. Finally, he assesses the failures of modern politico-economic systems and considers what simpler societies can teach complex ones about protecting social welfare and improving interpersonal relationships.

Mauss achieves his principal objectives in *The Gift*. The main arguments are backed up by a good deal of empirical evidence (evidence verifiable by observation). However, the conclusions are more speculative due to the lack of comparable data on industrialized societies.

Approach

To analyze the middle level of social evolution*—according to which societies advance in recognizable states to increased sophistication—Mauss hypothesizes an earlier phase in which individuality was completely subordinated to the family or clan.* Groups were bound to each other by systems of "*préstations totales*" or "total services." These included all things exchanged between them: goods, courtesies, marriage partners, meals, and intangibles such as dances, titles, names, and rituals.

Mauss explains that the gift exchange systems of existing and historical archaic societies* developed out of the total services system but involve larger territories and higher-order political units such as tribes.* Trade* (the formalized exchange of unalike items according to prescribed standards of value) and barter* (the exchange of dissimilar items on the spot and possibly involving bargaining) occur alongside gift exchange, reflecting the emergence of individual personhood.* In complex agricultural and industrial societies, individuality develops further as family and social bonds weaken due to modern forms of anonymous transactions mediated by abstract currency.[1]

Mauss illustrates the system of total services through examples such as thanksgiving feasts and gift sacrifice in Polynesia,* Australia and New Zealand, Malaysia, the far north of Eurasia, Africa, and the Americas. He then describes a class of competitive gift cycles he names after the *potlatch** system of feasts along the Northwest Coast of North America, a means to display wealth in which increasingly expensive gifts were handed over, and objects sometimes destroyed.

Mauss explains that comparable systems are common in Papua New Guinea and elsewhere in Melanesia.* In addition, many seemingly elementary systems of total services are really intermediate forms marked by escalation.[2] Such mild *potlatch* systems exist in Australia, Fiji, southern Asia, and among what he calls the Pygmies.* Traces remain in the laws and customs of ancient Rome, India, Germanic populations, and China.[3]

Lastly, Mauss analyzes "survivals" (enduring traces of ancient ideas or practices) in languages and laws derived from ancient Semitic, Greek, Roman, Indian, Germanic, Celtic, and Chinese civilizations. He shows that reciprocity and social institutions continue to sustain old systems of obligation and entitlement through gifts. However, in complex society individuality prevails due to the predominance of exchange formalized through money and contract law.

Contribution in Context

Mauss's analysis generated original insights about gift exchange and social relationships across ethnographic settings. To illustrate, Mauss provides a unified explanation for the competitive escalating systems of feasts and gifts that he describes as "*prestations totales agonistique.*" These include the *kula** ring, by which wealth objects move among the Trobriand Islands, and the *potlatch* system of feasts on the Northwest Coast of North America.

The kula described by Bronislaw Malinowski* involves the circulation of decorated white shell armbands and red shell disc necklaces carried by canoe in opposite directions from one Trobriand island to another.[4] There is bartering for everyday goods but only the gift objects carry invisible spiritual qualities, confer prestige rather than use value, and are paid back after a time lag. The value of the armbands and necklaces rises by having been previously held by esteemed people such as respected "big men," and is independent of their aesthetic qualities.

Likewise, the gifts exchanged through the Northwest Coast potlatch system of feasts described by Franz Boas* carry spiritual force. Copper is especially valued because it attracts other copper objects. The potlatch is unique for its extremes of competitiveness. To really "flatten" a rival chief and tribe, the hosts may destroy huge amounts of their own valuable property: blankets, food, houses, and copper objects thrown into the sea. Here Mauss shows how gifts that cannot be returned increase the prestige of the giver and humiliate the receiver.[5]

Mauss shows how these different gift cycles express the same patterns of moral and material transfer. He identifies the distinction already present in simpler societies between one-off commodity transactions and gifts in which the individual and larger society are involved.[6] Mauss's comparative analysis reveals that the flow of transfers is orderly and meaningful in all societies.

NOTES

1   Marcel Mauss, *The Gift: The Form and Reason for Exchange in Archaic Societies* (London: Routledge, 1990), 5–6, 46, 82–3.

2   Mauss, *The Gift*, 7.

3   Mauss, *The Gift*, 7, 19, 97–8.

4   Bronislaw Malinowski, *Argonauts of the Western Pacific: An Account of Native Enterprise and Adventure in the Archipelagos of Melanesian New Guinea* (London: Routledge, 1922).

5   Mauss, *The Gift*, 37, 74, 86–8.

6   Mauss, *The Gift*, 11.

SECTION 2
IDEAS

MODULE 5
MAIN IDEAS

KEY POINTS

- Mauss shows that gifts are not simply presents given out of generosity but tools for building social relationships. The obligations carried by gift exchange connect people in positive and negative ways.

- Gift exchange is what makes face-to-face societies tick: it fuels and structures economic, social, religious, and political life. Gift cycles either create mutual obligations or, if interrupted, result in gains in honor and status for the donor at the expense of the receiver.

- Mauss demonstrates how reciprocal exchanges bind individuals and groups but also protect their autonomy, whereas commercial transactions are more favorable to exploitation. The balance between the two influences the level of social cohesiveness and the quality of human interactions.

Key Themes

The focus of Marcel Mauss's analysis in *The Gift* is small-scale or archaic societies* throughout the world but especially in the Pacific region of Melanesia,* Northwest North America, and ancient Eurasia. Mauss shows how the obligation to give, to receive, and, after a set period of time, to return gifts sustains long-term social relationships that bind individuals and groups in positive and negative ways. The force that compels exchange derives from unwritten but nonetheless formal legal principles, cultural beliefs about honor and prestige, and the symbolic meanings conveyed by the objects and nonmaterial goods that pass between parties. The blending of material, human, and

❝ What rule of legality and self-interest, in societies of a backward or archaic type, compels the gift that has been received to be obligatorily reciprocated? What power resides in the object given that causes its recipient to pay it back? **❞**

Marcel Mauss, *The Gift: The Form and Reason for Exchange in Archaic Societies*

magical or spiritual elements makes economic activity inseparable from social, religious, and political systems and relationships.

The fundamental principle behind the entire system of gift exchange is the concept that "one good turn deserves another," or reciprocity.* It is the same idea behind the expression, "there's no such thing as a free lunch." These "survivals" of an earlier historical period in European and American culture seem to show that regardless of what sort of society people live in, gift-giving is a complicated process, with the gift itself full of all sorts of mixed messages and not necessarily a physical object. For example, even the very words "gift" and "present" might signify donations such as time and knowledge or talents such as musical ability.

Mauss focuses on how reciprocity contributes to social cohesion in small, face-to-face societies in which—unlike in market* societies where labor, land, goods, and services are calculated in units of currency—exchanges are characterized by personal and social meaning and obligation; these exchanges are, further, motivated by things such as prestige, duty, honor, sacrifice, generosity, and self-interest. The things that change hands include tangible goods (physical things such as jewelry, housewares, and clothing); food and drink, often shared between parties; and intangible things such as hospitality, dances, names, titles, and rituals. Gifts must be returned with equivalent or better gifts, which may be something completely different to the original gift. In all cases gifts are calculated according to established systems of value, which include qualities that may or may not embrace utilitarian considerations. The sum total of these laws and rules is nothing less than a map of the society and its connections to others.[1]

Exploring the Ideas

Basing his analysis on gift exchange, Mauss shows that culture plays a major role in shaping human behavior. In contrast to the then-current notion that social features were determined by ecological, material, and biological factors, Mauss focuses on social institutions* and cultural beliefs or collective representations* (shared beliefs and understandings) as he did in earlier work on magic and religion. Through the "total social phenomenon" or "total social fact" of gift exchange, Mauss illustrates Émile Durkheim's* belief that the institutions of simple societies serve to maintain social stability and solidarity.* Therefore, social cohesiveness (the closeness of relationships among members of a society) requires that individuals accept being constrained in their behavior by systematic and long-term obligations to others. Reciprocal exchange, however, still allows individuals to exercise self-interest.

Gift cycles hold small, face-to-face societies together, even while revealing and reinforcing hierarchies and inequalities between and within them. Continuous reciprocal exchange is the opposite of discrete sales mediated by money and moneyless transactions through barter* (the exchange of dissimilar items) or trade* (the formalized exchange of dissimilar items according to prescribed standards of value). In other words, the contrast is between reciprocal exchange, which involves open-ended time scales and items whose values are not reckoned in terms of currency, and one-time exchanges where values are balanced either because, for instance, a certain number of bananas is worth a certain number of shells, or there is currency to do the work of translating commodity values into units. Mauss also shows that trade is not unknown to simple societies and that credit is built into the gift cycle through ratcheting values and delayed repayment, which is like interest. In sum, economic activity, including gift exchange, is structured according to similar principles across all kinds of societies.

Mauss suggests that comparing and contrasting gift exchange across various societies highlights principles that can guide us all and lead to a better society, and that indicate that not all progress is positive.[2] In advanced civilizations, where economics is seen as a straightforward matter of cash and contract, people fail to recognize and cultivate reciprocity. People in Western societies, he says, are more isolated, whereas people in simpler societies are more interconnected but nonetheless maintain their autonomy. The point is that the Western system does not promote reciprocal material and spiritual exchange to the degree it could. As a result, people are more distanced from one another, and there is lower social solidarity. Mauss applauds the simpler groups and populations who "have learnt how to oppose and to give to one another without sacrificing themselves to one another," concluding that this is "what tomorrow, in our so-called civilized world, classes and nations and individuals also, must learn. This is one of the enduring secrets of their wisdom and solidarity."[3]

Language and Expression
The Gift is a deceptively short essay of around one hundred pages of text complemented by a roughly equal quantity of notes. The essay first appeared in 1923–4 in *L'Année Sociologique.** Publication of the journal had been suspended since World War I* due to the deaths of several main contributors including the journal's founder, Durkheim. Mauss had collaborated with this group on a variety of projects and was determined to carry their collective scholarly legacy forward. His contribution to the revived journal speaks to an audience that would have included them, had they been alive.

The original title of *The Gift* was *Essai sur le don: forme et raison de l'échange dans les sociétés archaïques—Essay on the Gift: The Form and Reason of Exchange in Archaic Societies*. Mauss's choice of the word "essay" reflects his intention to present an argument in a concise and orderly, but not overly academic, way. But the work is written for people who already have a basic knowledge of early twentieth-century sociology and anthropology.* For today's readers, previous knowledge of contemporary sociological theory and the ethnographic* material discussed in the book is helpful but not necessary. The notes help fill in the picture.

The 1954 English translation is very much written in the formal language of the day, whereas the 1990 translation cited in this analysis is a less close fit to the spirit and content of the original.[4]

NOTES

1   Mary Douglas, "Foreword: No Free Gifts," in *The Gift* by Marcel Mauss (London: Routledge, 2000), VIII.

2   Marcel Mauss, *The Gift: The Form and Reason for Exchange in Archaic Societies* (London: Routledge, 1990), 77.

3   Mauss, *The Gift*, 82–3.

4   For an illustration, see the two translations of Mauss's sentence beginning with "Les clans, les âges et, généralement, les sexes." Marcel Mauss, "Essai sur le Don: Forme et Raison de l'Échange dans les Sociétés Archaïques," *L'Année Sociologique* no. 1 (1923–4): 97; Marcel Mauss, *The Gift: Forms and Functions of Exchange in Archaic Societies* (Glencoe, IL: Free Press (1954), 70; Marcel Mauss, *The Gift: The Form and Reason for Exchange in Archaic Societies* (London: Routledge, 1990), 72.

MODULE 6
SECONDARY IDEAS

KEY POINTS

- In addition to the political and legal structures that sustain social relationships built through gift exchange, Mauss identifies a transcendent quality of gifts (a quality that cannot be quantified in exclusively physical terms) that motivates people to keep them in circulation.

- Cultural beliefs about the mystical properties of gifts favor compliance and therefore social solidarity* and stability. While reciprocal* exchange maintains hierarchies within and between societies, gift cycles involving spiritual beings demand transfers to the poor that buffer the effects of inequality.

- Mauss shows that supernatural elements of gift and commercial transactions persist in complex societies. He provides a model for investigating the implicit motivations and meanings embedded in economic behavior everywhere.

Other Ideas

In *The Gift*, Marcel Mauss proposes that local variants of the Pacific Polynesian* and Melanesian* concept of *mana** explain how archaic cultures* infuse gifts with religious, spiritual, and magical forces. In *A General Theory of Magic*, a 1904 publication written with the historian and sociologist Henri Hubert,* Mauss explains that these concepts refer to a spiritual force that pervades the universe.[1] Throughout the southern Pacific, Africa, Asia, the Americas, and the Middle East, archaic societies attribute power and advantages to the *mana* attached to objects and possessions, and, through them, to people. To illustrate

❝ Thus [Maori gifts] contain within them that force, in cases where the law, particularly the obligation to reciprocate, may fail to be observed. ❞

Marcel Mauss, *The Gift: The Form and Reason for Exchange in Archaic Societies*

the *mana*-like qualities of gifts, Mauss describes the Maori*— indigenous New Zealand—concept of *hau*,* or the power of a class of gifts that carries them back to their place of origin. Where political and legal structures, honor, and concern for social status fail, the spirit of the gift itself ensures that it will continue to circulate.[2]

Mauss draws an analogy between these beliefs and alms (charitable gifts) as a form of gift exchange with the spirits, a topic covered in "Essai sur la Nature et la Fonction du Sacrifice," his 1898 work with Henri Hubert on the role of sacrifice in ancient religions.[3] Just as sacrificial offerings are given to the spirits in recognition of their gifts to humans and as a way to attract future benefits, through alms to the poor the better-off demonstrate awareness of their place in the cycle of exchange that is the source of their wealth and good fortune. Mauss cites beliefs about almsgiving as a principle of justice and obligation under the threat of divine retribution in Christianity and Islam and among the Hausa (an ethnic Sub-Saharan people) of the northeast African nation of Sudan, the ancient Semites and Hindus, and Arab cultures.

The spiritual grease for the wheels of exchange furnished by concepts such as *mana* and *hau*, as well as their relation to alms, supports Mauss's principal ideas about the obligatory nature of gift cycles. Mauss argues that rich members of industrialized societies should be reminded of their custodial role vis-à-vis the poor. The blessing of overabundance demands to be acknowledged through redistribution.

Exploring the Ideas

Mauss explains that gifts are alive; they carry something of the person or people who held them previously; and they insist on continued movement. To illustrate, he analyzes the Maori concept of *hau* that pertains primarily to objects known as *taonga*, gifts passed along maternal lines such as mats, decorations, and talismans. These are defined as fixed property linked to its place of origin, in contrast to *oloa* or movable objects such as tools. While *taonga* items may be traded for other things such as food in ordinary transactions, when given as gifts, *hau* demands that they be returned on pain of serious, potentially mortal, harm to the holder.

The *taonga* "is animated by the *hau* of its forest, its native heath and soil."[4] Moreover, the *taonga* carries some part of the person who gives it: "The *taonga* or its *hau* … is attached to this chain of users until these give back … by way of feasts, festivals, and presents, the equivalent or something of even greater value. This in turn will give the donors authority and power over the first donor, who has become the last recipient. This is the key idea that in Samoa and New Zealand seems to dominate the obligatory circulation of wealth, tribute, and gifts."[5]

Mauss suggests that for many simple societies gifts *are living things*, not a metaphor for them. Referring to ancient Hindu laws, he explains: "The land, the food, and all that one gives are, moreover, personified: they are living creatures with whom one enters into a dialogue, and who share in the contract. They seek to be given away."[6]

Similarly, in Germany and France contracts involving sales and loans are accompanied by a personal object of little value that is "infused with the individuality of the donor" and returned upon completion of the deal.[7] This tradition derives from the earlier practice of cutting a pledge object in two for the contracting parties to keep and by which they exerted power over one another.

These examples illustrate Mauss's point that the spiritual quality of gifts supplies what legal strictures cannot: a psychological motivation rooted in supernatural awe.

Overlooked

The idea that mystical forces infuse the world around us, including gifts, has not been received with the same enthusiasm as Mauss's main framework for analyzing the legal and cultural systems behind reciprocal* exchange. One reason is that evidence for analogous concepts to *mana* and *hau* is relatively scarce in *The Gift*.[8] Another reason is that Western society's scientific mindset and monotheistic religions—faith in a single god—are contrary to the idea of a world enchanted by supernatural forces. This world view is consistent with utilitarianism,* a philosophical theory founded by the British philosopher Jeremy Bentham* and strongly associated with the philosopher John Stuart Mill's* writings on the central importance of individual potential and responsibility. Utilitarianism takes for granted an individualistic human nature that drives people to make rational* choices based on utility*—that is, costs and benefits are weighed and decisions are made on the practical consequence of that choice. Unless there is interference by society or the state, individual actions add up to growth and opportunity for the benefit of all.[9]

Durkheim* and Mauss rejected utilitarianism in favor of a focus on social forces. Their approach makes it possible to see that cultures define utility and rationality in different ways, including ones that account for social and spiritual relationships. Since then the influence of utilitarianism has ebbed and flowed through popular culture and political philosophy. It has found new life in the economic school of neoliberalism (an economic philosophy of the late twentieth and early twenty-first centuries that revives nineteenth-century liberalism's* emphasis on economic growth through free-market principles and law-based governance free of interference in individual liberties) and in new forms of social Darwinism (the use of evolutionary theory to explain the different traits and fortunes of individuals or groups of people as a consequence of their biological inferiority or superiority). These ideas are based on assumptions of human nature as definable by self-interest, and the naturalness of utilitarian market* exchange—that the economic marketplace, which operates according to the exercise of selfishness, is somehow natural.

While Mauss's insights into the mystical elements of reciprocal exchange may be considered secondary to his principal arguments, they have not been entirely overlooked. Scholars and critics examine why wealthy individuals give to charity and spend large sums on art and other non-utilitarian possessions, as Mauss notes. They question whether conspicuous consumption concerns something more than class-climbing in the nineteenth-century sense described by the US sociologist and economist Thorstein Veblen.*[10] Researchers have identified spiritual or magical beliefs in organ donation, because biological gifts are often seen as alive with the donor's personhood*— and so impose obligations on recipients and their families.[11]

NOTES

1   Marcel Mauss and Henri Hubert, *A General Theory of Magic* (London: Routledge, 2001).

2   Marcel Mauss, *The Gift: The Form and Reason for Exchange in Archaic Societies* (London: Routledge, 1990), 8–13.

3   Marcel Mauss and Henri Hubert, "Essai sur la Nature et la Fonction du Sacrifice," *L'Année Sociologique* (1897–8): 29–138.

4   Mauss, *The Gift*, 11–12.

5   Mauss, *The Gift*, 12.

6   Mauss, *The Gift*, 56.

7   Mauss, *The Gift*, 62.

8   Seth Leacock, "The Ethnological Theory of Marcel Mauss," *American Anthropologist* 56 (1954): 63–4.

9   Marshall Sahlins, *The Western Illusion of Human Nature: With Reflections on the Long History of Hierarchy, Equality and the Sublimation of Anarchy in the West, and Comparative Notes on Other Conceptions of the Human Condition* (Chicago: Prickly Paradigm Press, 2008).

10 Thorstein Veblen, *The Theory of the Leisure Class: An Economic Study of the Evolution of Institutions* (New York: MacMillan, 1899).

11 Lesley A. Sharp, "Commodified Kin: Death, Mourning, and Competing Claims on the Bodies of Organ Donors in the United States," *American Anthropologist* 103, no. 1 (2001): 112–33.

MODULE 7
ACHIEVEMENT

KEY POINTS

- Mauss shows that the binding obligations inherent in gift cycles project social relationships into the future. He extends the principle that economic transactions are socially regulated and culturally meaningful from societies without money to those that run on market* principles (with the economic exchange of goods based on established calculated values).

- The analysis brings together the ethnographic* research of other scholars with Mauss's own interpretations of ancient laws and literature, which he read in the original languages.

- Mauss convincingly draws parallels between gifts and commercial transactions in existing and historical archaic societies.* He is less successful with regard to implications for industrialized societies due to a scarcity of relevant empirical data.

Assessing the Argument

Marcel Mauss's comparison of reciprocal* exchange systems in small societies in *The Gift* shows how combined, collective representations* (shared beliefs and understandings) and social institutions* (formalized relationships or activities such as retirement or marriage) define social interaction and channel human behavior in specific ways. In addition to legal frameworks, the moral and mystical baggage attached to gifts ensures that they will be returned or passed on, often with increase and according to a predetermined time frame. Trade* and barter* occur alongside these "systems of total prestation" (that is, customary

> ❝ Men had learnt how to pledge their honour and their name long before they knew how to sign the latter. ❞
>
> Marcel Mauss, *The Gift: The Form and Reason for Exchange in Archaic Societies*

payment). Goods such as blankets, fish, yams, and copper objects carry fixed values in relation to each other, and repayment can involve a delay. In some cases there is currency* such as shells, pieces of metal, and coins belonging to individuals or clans.* In all of these societies there are concepts of purchasing power, debt, and credit, just as there are in modern societies.[1]

Mauss argues that the reverse is also true: archaic gift cycles persist in modern market economies. This is evident in laws, literature, and the obligation to return invitations. It explains gambling and other exchanges involving honor and theoretically voluntary, but obligatory, payment, and the fact that "Charity is still wounding for him who has accepted it."[2]

However, redistribution now occurs through taxes and legislative processes, which interrupt the cycle of exchange that puts people's honor at stake. While anonymous transactions are not simply the outcome of individual rational* choices separate from cultural values, it is difficult to assess the symbolic and social meaning of spending behavior. Likewise, more evidence is needed to demonstrate that a higher proportion of gift versus commercial exchanges correlates with a higher level of social cohesion.

These limitations mean that Mauss can only offer recommendations for the modern world. He suggests combining lessons from archaic societies with individuality, market principles, and the will to work. In this way, complex societies can prevent the exploitation of the poor, more fully compensate laborers through social protections, and acknowledge that it is never possible or even desirable to completely fulfill an obligation.[3]

Achievement in Context

Mauss was not the first to examine economic exchange as a socially ordered phenomenon governed by cultural beliefs or collective representations. In *The Philosophy of Money* in 1907 the German philosopher and sociologist* Georg Simmel* analyzed economic systems in relation to social interaction and symbolic meanings, and showed that the value of things is changeable and socially constructed.[4] *The Protestant Ethic and the Spirit of Capitalism*, pioneering sociologist Max Weber's* 1904–5 analysis of the rise of capitalism* in Europe, traced connections between religious beliefs, economic organization, and individual behavior;[5] capitalism is the economic and social model, founded on the private ownership of industry and business, dominant in the West (and increasingly throughout the Western world) today.

Mauss's work was distinctive in its focus on archaic societies across great spans of time and space. Mauss shifted the focus on the social and cultural shaping of economic behavior to transactions that occur in the absence of money and under the guise of gifts. *The Gift* took the study of total social phenomena to a different level.

The essay was first published in 1923–4 in French in the journal *L'Année Sociologique,* * and was not translated into English until 30 years later. The lack of a translation and the essay's publication in a scholarly journal limited its accessibility outside the circle of intellectuals capable of reading multiple European languages. These same readers would have been familiar with the Durkheimian* school of sociology as well as the work of Simmel and Weber.

Within these limits, *The Gift* was influential from the start. In addition to exploring a unique theme through a novel approach, the essay appeared after a long lull in publication of *L'Année Sociologique* and was written by one of Durkheim's successors. The book's contribution to the development of British structural-functionalism* was ensured through scholars whose ethnographic writings were its source material, including A. R. Radcliffe-Brown* and Bronislaw Malinowski.*

Although the anthropologist* Raymond Firth,* a scholar of indigenous New Zealand cultures, disputed the way Mauss interpreted the data he had collected among the Maori,* the book's influence was not affected by concerns over the quality of the evidence used.[6] Those concerns emerged decades later, when scholars began to rethink the premises behind fieldwork conducted by previous generations of researchers. The circumstances framing ethnographic encounters and the attitudes and abilities of researchers came under fire, bringing a reevaluation of the validity of their findings.

Limitations

Mauss's analysis of gift exchange as a social institution underpinned by a bundle of collective representations concerning obligation, honor, and, in at least some cases, supernatural forces, has passed the test of time. Although some of its ideas have been cast aside, the book's impact has not been limited by the subject matter, theoretical approach, or linkage to a single time or place. Even the whole set of nomadic foraging* (hunter-gatherer) societies unknown to Mauss show some of the characteristics and dynamics he identified in relation to settled foragers of the Northwest Coast of North America and village-based agriculturalists studied by ethnographers throughout the world in the late nineteenth and early twentieth centuries.

The text has not been severely challenged since its publication. Even after social evolutionary* theory (founded on the idea that societies progress through a fixed series of stages of ever-increasing technological, social, and intellectual perfection) and structural-functionalism (a theory that focuses on the ways in which societies are structured and in which their internal parts are integrated with one another) lost favor along with the method of comparative analysis,* *The Gift* remained a foundational text across many disciplines. Mauss's partial acceptance of the prevalent evolutionary doctrines of his time did not fundamentally distort his analysis. His comparative method was thorough and well grounded in a comprehensive analysis of beliefs and practices in context, in contrast to the opportunistic use of ethnographic research on the part of evolutionists intent upon arranging social facts in a predetermined classificatory scheme.

Mauss and Durkheim have been criticized for their alleged failure to consider individuals and social change. However, although they focused on collective representations and social institutions, they also thought about individual personhood* and the relationship between social norms and individual belief and action. They had a theory of change that is implicit in Mauss's analysis of shifts in systems of gift exchange in step with changes in politico-economic organization.[7]

The Gift is relevant not only to anthropology and sociology but disciplines across the humanities and social sciences, including linguistics, economics, history, philosophy, and political science. The book continues to provide a basis for analyzing past and present behavior and social norms. It transmits ethnographic portraits of an earlier age that might otherwise be forgotten.

NOTES

1 Marcel Mauss, *The Gift: The Form and Reason for Exchange in Archaic Societies* (London: Routledge, 1990), 36, 100–1.

2 Mauss, *The Gift*, 65, 112.

3 Mary Douglas, "Foreword: No Free Gifts," in *The Gift* by Marcel Mauss (London: Routledge, 2000), xv.

4 Georg Simmel, *The Philosophy of Money* (London: Routledge, 1978).

5 Max Weber, *The Protestant Ethic and the Spirit of Capitalism: The Relationships between Religion and the Economic and Social Life in Modern Culture* (New York: Charles Scribner's Sons, 1958).

6 Raymond Firth, *Primitive Economics of the New Zealand Maori* (London: Routledge, 1929).

7 Douglas, "Foreword: No Free Gifts"; Seth Leacock, "The Ethnological Theory of Marcel Mauss," *American Anthropologist* 56 (1954): 58–71.

MODULE 8
PLACE IN THE AUTHOR'S WORK

KEY POINTS

- Marcel Mauss's teaching, writing, and political engagement were unified by a focus on the social norms, shared beliefs, and legal structures that direct human interaction and influence social solidarity.*

- *The Gift* exemplifies Mauss's approach: the essay integrates earlier ethnological* comparisons (comparisons drawn from the study of ethnographic material*) and sociological* theories with reflections on the positive and negative sides of modern civilization.

- *The Gift* was Mauss's last major comparative analysis* and his most significant scholarly contribution. His later work remained consistent with its premises and approach.

Positioning

The foundational anthropologist* Claude Lévi-Strauss* calls *The Gift* Marcel Mauss's "masterpiece" and "most deservedly famous" publication;[1] the US anthropologist Walter Goldschmidt* says it is Mauss's "most important noncollaborative effort."[2] The book is emblematic of the transition between nineteenth-century positivism and twentieth-century social anthropology ushered in by Émile Durkheim* and his associates in the years before World War I.* Positivism is a scientific system established by the French philosopher Auguste Comte to unify disciplines from mathematics to sociology through the same basic principles and standards of evidence.

Throughout his career, Mauss collaborated frequently, taught and learned as a lifelong student, and mixed intellectual and political writing. Mauss preferred to concentrate on "his materials" as opposed

> **❝** In this concrete observation of social life lies the means of discovering new facts, which we are only beginning dimly to perceive. In our opinion, nothing is more urgent or more fruitful than this study of total social facts. **❞**
>
> Marcel Mauss, *The Gift: The Form and Reason for Exchange in Archaic Societies*

to engaging in theoretical debates or defending cherished dogma. He built bridges with other scholars, was not stopped by disciplinary boundaries, and avoided clashes by sticking to Durkheim's positivist emphasis on empirical (that is, verifiable) evidence. The French anthropologist Maurice Leenhardt* sums up Mauss's contribution: "Few books, articles dispersed everywhere, an enormous influence."[3]

In addition to *The Gift*, Mauss's body of work includes his studies on magic, religion, money, mourning customs, suicide, Bolshevism* (the political movement on which the Soviet Union* was originally founded) and violence. For the journal *L'Année Sociologigue** Mauss contributed short pieces and book reviews, and edited numerous unfinished works by Durkheim and other scholars. In addition, collections of Mauss's writings on methodology, sociology, and politics were published in his final years and after his death in 1950.[4]

Mauss's productivity diminished after publication of *The Gift*, due to the deaths of many of his closest associates during World War I* and the political turbulence of the interwar period. Mauss diverted his energies to political activism and institutional development in the French university system. He left several unfinished manuscripts on topics including Bolshevism, prayer, the nation, and technology.[5]

Many of the topics and empirical evidence discussed in *The Gift* appear in Mauss's previous writings on religion, magic, and the social organization of seasonal productive activity. Mauss's political activism trained his attention on legal systems and the political dimensions of exchange. Although he valued the comparative method, Mauss remained committed throughout his career to the view that social phenomena must be studied in their entire context. In sum, the wide range of his interests matched Mauss's lifelong goal of understanding societies in themselves, in relation to one another, and over time.

Integration

Claude Lévi-Strauss explains that Mauss was ahead of his time in realizing that "the mental and the social are one and the same."[6] In 1926, Mauss reported on cultural beliefs that result in mortal harm to individuals, reflecting his appreciation of the society–body–mind nexus—that is, the whole formed by the combination of these things.[7] A 1934 paper, "Les Techniques du Corps," examined the imprinting of cultural beliefs on small children through the management of bodily processes.[8] The American anthropologist Ruth Benedict's* comparative analysis of indigenous* populations in Melanesia,* New Mexico, and the Northwest Coast of North America appeared the same year. Together the two scholars helped develop an emerging discipline concerned with culture* and personality, mental ability, and psychological distress.[9]

At the same time, in some respects Mauss remained set in his ways. While he avoided using words such as "primitive" or "inferior," he nevertheless grouped societies according to their place on an evolutionary* progression throughout his career. In a 1938 lecture, Mauss discussed the evolution of individuality through the same ordering of ethnographic and historical sources presented in *The Gift*.[10]

The relationship between individuality on the one hand, and the ways in which economic behavior is constrained by non-economic institutions, social justice, and solidarity on the other, was a constant theme running through Mauss's work. In *The Gift*, Mauss explains that societies at a middle stage of social evolution* learned how to institutionalize gift relationships as a way to protect against shortages and avoid violence. This took the uncertainty and risk out of intergroup encounters typical of earlier stages of human history, in which the idea of individual personhood* barely existed.[11]

In middle-stage societies, trading for personal reasons arises alongside systems of obligation that channel prestige, honor, and exchange goods towards group leaders. In more advanced societies, individuality flourishes because money distances exchange relationships from their social and moral context. Traces of archaic exchange remain in forms such as charitable giving, worker consciousness of the inadequacy of wages as compensation for labor, and bank-breaking outlays of cash for ceremonial feasts. Mauss's scholarly and political interests come together in his view that these surviving elements of reciprocity* should be cultivated in order to promote justice, economic growth, and peace.

Significance

Mauss's most significant intellectual legacy is, without a doubt, *The Gift*. The book has been required reading for anthropology students for generations. It has inspired other comparative analyses and an enormous amount of research on reciprocity and exchange relationships. Although the book's social evolutionary premises have been abandoned and the comparative method severely challenged since its publication, Mauss's insights into collective representations* and the interrelationships among social, economic, political, and religious institutions* have remained compelling.

The book is a landmark text and a testament to Mauss's knowledge, linguistic abilities, and exacting scholarship. However, the book alone is not the basis for its author's reputation. Mauss was a political activist, a contributor to and editor of political and academic publications, the co-founder of academic institutes, and a teacher and lecturer. He shared his ideas with other scholars, coauthored many publications, and strengthened Durkheim's influence on the human sciences.

Although Durkheim left an enormous imprint on Mauss's thinking, which the latter gratefully acknowledged, Mauss's work took its own path. Unlike Durkheim, Mauss immersed himself in the political struggles of his time and drew connections to his academic work. Nonetheless the two are often criticized together for ignoring individuals in favor of disembodied social facts and presuming a tight, stable fit between collective representations and social institutions. The British scholar Mary Douglas,* however, says that Durkheim and Mauss both considered the role of individual minds in generating and maintaining collective representations, and were not uninterested in change. For example, the line of argumentation in *The Gift* reflects an underlying theory of social change by which economic transactions shift from gift to contract.[12]

Although grounded in his uncle's sociological tradition, Mauss's reputation and impact derive from his own particular focus and findings. *The Gift* exemplifies Mauss's conviction that comparison based on reliable, detailed, contextualized data about "total social facts" is the key to understanding human societies and individual behavior.

NOTES

1   Seth Leacock, "The Ethnological Theory of Marcel Mauss," *American Anthropologist* 56 (1954): 65; Marcel Fournier, *Marcel Mauss: A Biography* (Princeton, NJ: Princeton University Press, 2005), 1.

2   Walter Goldschmidt, "Untitled Review of *The Gift* by Marcel Mauss," *American Anthropologist* 57, no. 6 (1955): 1299.

3   Fournier, *Marcel Mauss*, 4.

4   Marcel Mauss, *Manuel d'Ethnographie* (Paris: Payot, 1947); Marcel Mauss, *Sociologie et Anthropologie* (Paris: Presses Universaires de France, 1950).

5   Fournier, *Marcel Mauss;* Goldschmidt, "Untitled Review"; Leacock, "The Ethnological Theory."

6   Claude Lévi-Strauss, *Introduction to the Work of Marcel Mauss* (London: Routledge and Kegan Paul, 1987), 21.

7   Marcel Mauss "Effet Physique chez l'Individu de l'Idée de Mort Suggérée par la Collectivité," *Journal de Psychologie Normale et Pathologique* XXIII, no. 6 (1926): 653–9.

8   Marcel Mauss, "Les Techniques du Corps," *Journal de Psychologie Normale et Pathologique* XXXII, nos 3–4 (1934): 271–93.

9   Lévi-Strauss, *Introduction*, 3–8, 11–13.

10 Marcel Mauss, "Une Catégorie de l'Esprit Humain," *Journal of the Royal Anthropological Institute* XLVIII, no. 2 (1938): 263–81; Leacock, "The Ethnological Theory," 69–70.

11 Marcel Mauss, *The Gift: The Form and Reason for Exchange in Archaic Societies* (London: Routledge, 1990).

12 Mary Douglas, "Foreword: No Free Gifts," in *The Gift* by Marcel Mauss (London: Routledge, 2000).

SECTION 3
IMPACT

MODULE 9
THE FIRST RESPONSES

KEY POINTS

- *The Gift* has been criticized mainly for overstating the continuity among concepts and practices across cultures. Critics also argue that the book's evolutionary framework ties it and its author more to the past than the future of anthropology* and sociology.*

- Mauss's supporters argue that his analysis in *The Gift* was methodologically sound and empirically accurate (that is, founded on verifiable evidence). They point out that his other work on mind–body connections and the interrelated social and biological spheres of human existence was ahead of its time.

- The 30-year time lag before translation into English was a major factor in the book's reception. By the 1950s, social evolutionism* and comparative analysis* had fallen out of favor in anthropology, leading to *The Gift* being criticized on both accounts.

Criticism

Most of the scholars cited by Marcel Mauss in *The Gift*, including Bronislaw Malinowski* and Franz Boas,* reacted positively to the book.[1] The anthropologist Raymond Firth,* an expert on indigenous New Zealand culture, however, questioned the originality of the analysis and disputed Mauss's interpretation of Maori* customs and concepts.[2]

After the author's death and the book's publication in English in 1954, *The Gift* was criticized by a generation of anthropologists who were wary of the search for general laws, the progressive logic of

> 66 The sense of work in common, as a team, the conviction that collaboration is a force against isolation, against the pretentious search for originality, may be what characterizes my scientific career, even more now perhaps than before. 99

Marcel Mauss, "L'Oeuvre de Mauss par lui-même"

evolutionism, and the method of comparative analysis. They argued that Mauss overemphasized similarities in institutions* across cultures* and ignored or downplayed differences, possibly as a result of his lack of fieldwork experience.[3] More, they criticized Mauss for disapproving of the English anthropologist J. G. Frazer* for presuming the universality of totemism* (the practice of infusing a neutral object with sacredness as the symbol for a group of people) without evidence, while extending terms such as *potlatch** and *mana** (a spiritual force potentially attached to objects) to the institutions of societies where parallel, local concepts were lacking.[4] *Potlatch* was a ceremonial feast practiced by Native American populations in Northwest North America that includes gifts to the guests; it was a means for the competitive display of wealth and prestige that even included the destruction of objects.

Even though Mauss discussed self-aggrandizement and the desire to belittle rivals, critics argued that he underplayed negative elements because they complicated the larger message that reciprocity* is necessary for social cohesion. Walter Goldschmidt* noted that his own studies of societies in Mauss's middle-range category revealed very clearly the greed, unscrupulousness, and "cold reasoning" involved in reciprocal exchange relationships.[5]

Finally, the knowledge that the institutions of simple societies are not just precursors to those of complex societies has called into question the value of evolutionary stages as a useful tool for

investigating and interpreting human societies. This had led many
critics to dismiss Mauss's conclusions about how to improve human
interaction in modern societies by expanding upon what's left of
surviving forms of reciprocity.

Responses

On the one hand, Mauss oriented his work according to a social
evolutionary framework throughout his career, as seen in his 1938
publication on the evolution of autonomous individuality.[6] On the
other hand, although he and Émile Durkheim* wrote in 1901 that,
once scientifically described, social facts became simply data for
comparative analysis, Mauss taught all his life that contextualization
(considering information in its social and environmental context) is
the necessary basis of well-founded cross-cultural knowledge.[7] He did
not take comparison lightly. To illustrate, in *The Gift*, he states that it
would be "too easy and too dangerous" to speculate about the
migration or independent origin of customs. "For the time being, it
must suffice to show the nature and very widespread diffusion of what
is a legal theme. Let others write its history, if they can."[8]

In spite of having applied ideas from his study of gift exchange to
European economies with the goal of making modern societies less
impersonal and individualistic, in 1930 Mauss was wary of ethical
conclusions drawn from ethnological comparisons. When it came to
the idea of the absorption of all cultures into a global monoculture,
Mauss "cautioned against applying value judgments to this trend, since
it, as well as 'progress,' cannot be shown to lead necessarily to good or
to happiness."[9] While unflagging in his moral and institutional support
for members of the Collège de Sociologie, which met in Paris from
1937 to 1939—especially the French thinkers Georges Bataille* and
Roger Caillois*—Mauss did not approve of the way they applied his
ideas from *The Gift* to their analysis of the sacred* in modern society.[10]

These critical responses to *The Gift* may partly explain why the book was Mauss's last large comparative analysis. After *The Gift* his attention shifted to topics such as psychological phenomena and political questions explored through a sociological perspective. None of this subsequent scholarship led Mauss to alter the original version of *The Gift*.

Conflict and Consensus

The originality of Mauss's work has been questioned—but, as he wrote in 1930, originality did not really interest him.[11] He was more concerned with collaboration, the analysis of concrete data, and cross-disciplinary thinking. Mauss practiced what he preached about reciprocity: he was kind, generous, and committed to sharing ideas and materials with others. As a result he published fewer manuscripts than he might have done, and *The Gift* stands out as one of the few he wrote alone.

There is no disagreement about Mauss's contribution to anthropological understanding of the ways that economic systems are embedded in broader social systems that encompass politics, kinship,* and religion. For instance, the 1940 work of the influential British anthropologist E. E. Evans-Pritchard,* who wrote the introduction to *The Gift*'s 1954 translation, described marriage payments among the Nuer people of southern Sudan as a "strand in the total circulation of cattle, and wives, and children, and men: every single relationship had its substantiation in a gift."[12]

As the "father of French ethnography,"* Mauss left an undisputed mark on the practice of anthropological research.[13] Although he did not have personal experience and saw fieldwork in terms of a brief expedition as opposed to long-term immersion, Mauss taught a precise, thorough method of data collection.[14] This is evident in the lectures he gave at the Institut d'Ethnologie from 1926 to 1939, and the fieldwork of students such as the sociologist Henri Lévy-Bruhl.*[15]

Mauss's work has inspired generations of those conducting

research in the field to map out reciprocal transfers as a point of access to interlinked sociopolitical institutions.[16] In *Elementary Forms of Kinship*, Claude Lévi-Strauss* describes transfers of men, women, and children as gifts in a network of mutual obligation and symbolic meaning. In other words, kinship* relations emerge through an integrated communication/exchange system.[17]

After the 1950s, scholars increasingly criticized the presumed objectivity and search for general laws embraced by Mauss and other followers of Durkheim. World events of the 1960s and 1970s contributed to a rethinking of the sources of knowledge, and these developments cast doubt on the validity of data gathered by earlier fieldworkers not trained to be critically aware of their own cultural biases.

NOTES

1 Marcel Fournier, *Marcel Mauss: A Biography* (Princeton, NJ: Princeton University Press, 2005), 244.

2 Firth argued that *hau* did not attach any element of the giver's personhood to the gift, although it did give the gift a life force. Barth points out that evidence from India supports Mauss's idea that something like *hau* explains the personhood carried by gifts in societies around the world. Fredrik Barth et al., *One Discipline, Four Ways: British, German, French, and American Anthropology* (Chicago: University of Chicago Press, 2005), 189; Raymond Firth, *Primitive Economics of the New Zealand Maori* (London: Routledge, 1929).

3 Seth Leacock, "The Ethnological Theory of Marcel Mauss," *American Anthropologist* 56 (1954): 59–60; Walter Goldschmidt, "Untitled Review of The Gift by Marcel Mauss," *American Anthropologist* 57, no. 6 (1955): 1299.

4 Leacock, "The Ethnological Theory," 63.

5 Goldschmidt, "Untitled Review," 1300.

6 Leacock, "The Ethnological Theory," 70.

7 Leacock, "The Ethnological Theory," 67.

8 Marcel Mauss, *The Gift: The Form and Reason for Exchange in Archaic*

Societies (London: Routledge, 1990), 98.

9   Leacock, "The Ethnological Theory," 64.

10   Fournier, *Marcel Mauss,* 327.

11   Marcel Mauss, "L'œuvre de Mauss par Lui-Même." *Revue Française de Sociologie* 20, nos 20–21 (1979): 209.

12   Mary Douglas, "Foreword: No Free Gifts," in *The Gift* by Marcel Mauss (London: Routledge, 2000), xv.

13   Georges Condominas, "Marcel Mauss, Père de l'ethnographie française," *Critique* 28, no. 297 (1972): 118–39.

14   Barth et al., *One Discipline, Four Ways,* 159.

15   Marcel Mauss, *Manuel d'ethnographie* (Paris: Payot, 1947).

16   Douglas, "Foreword: No Free Gifts," xii–xiii.

17   Claude Lévi-Strauss, *The Elementary Structures of Kinship* (Boston: Beacon Press, 1969); Douglas, "Foreword: No Free Gifts," xv.

MODULE 10
THE EVOLVING DEBATE

KEY POINTS

- Mauss has shown that exchanges that may seem invisible or inconsequential are central to human relationships and socioeconomic systems. This insight continues to inspire research on the link between open-ended reciprocity* and social cohesion in simple and complex societies.

- The book and the resulting critical dialogue has stimulated developments in the study of individual agency* (the capacity to act) in relation to social-structural constraints, comparative economic and political systems, and the production of knowledge.

- The book has had a mixed impact. It is a model of empirical richness and original insight into a complex phenomenon, but its evolutionary assumptions and insufficient attention to variability ground it in an earlier era and indicate hazards to avoid.

Uses and Problems

Marcel Mauss's most influential work, *The Gift* was part of an intellectual current that arose in France in opposition to British philosophy's utilitarian* theories of the eighteenth and nineteenth centuries, oriented toward the individual. Along with Émile Durkheim* and the rest of the group of scholars united around the journal *L'Année Sociologique,** Mauss sought to understand how society shaped the thoughts and behavior of individuals. These scholars explored the interaction between cultural beliefs and social institutions* and its connection to social solidarity.* Mauss contributed by showing how reciprocal exchange creates binding

68

> ❝ For the sheer range and imagination of his writings, which are nonetheless still rooted in the fairly well-delineated model drawn up by his uncle, Mauss has few peers. ❞
>
> Fredrik Barth,* *One Discipline, Four Ways: British, German, French, and American Anthropology*

social relationships that endure over time because gifts must be returned after a delay.

This current soon merged with the British theoretical approach of structural-functionalism,* which shared the basic assumption that the components of society work together to maintain stability and equilibrium. French structuralist* approaches under Claude Lévi-Strauss* were more specifically concentrated on explaining the way elements within myths, rituals, and stories were organized, how they related to one another, and what they expressed about culture and thought. All forms of structuralism came under fire in the 1960s and 1970s, as scholars questioned the totalizing force of collective representations* (shared beliefs and understandings), which they saw as too fixed and far removed from the minds of individuals acting in society.[1]

The focus shifted to discord and cultural dynamism. Symbolic or "interpretive" anthropologists led by Victor Turner* and Clifford Geertz,* known for their work in Africa and Indonesia respectively, explored myths, rituals, and symbols in motion through concrete situations; they examined social action, gaps and reversals in structure, and how meaning is constructed and embodied by individuals. The French sociologist Pierre Bourdieu* focused on power and its different vehicles such as social and symbolic capital, or forms of wealth such as reputation or control over knowledge that confer power similarly to financial assets. Bourdieu reintroduced the classical concept of habitus*—the embodiment of social and cultural conditions—that Mauss had explored in his 1934 work on the imprinting of social constructs on the body in childhood: "Les Techniques du Corps."[2] The linking of lived experience, inequalities of power, and language and culture* generated an enduring focus in social science on the ways in which sociocultural forces constrain individual agency (or the freedom and resources necessary for knowing and realizing one's own will).[3]

Schools of Thought

The interpretive, reflexive turn away from structuralism and functionalism occurred at the same time as troubling details emerged concerning the fieldwork conducted during the first half of the twentieth century. Clifford Geertz described how Malinowski's* diary revealed a physical and psychological detachment and cold, disdainful opinion of the "natives" expressed in coarse language.[4] The anthropologist Margaret Mead's* fieldwork in New Guinea was limited by an injured ankle and her lack of proficiency in indigenous* languages. These problems undermine her conclusions about different gender systems across three societies, which seem also to have been shaped by her personal life and professional agenda.[5] Lévi-Strauss likewise conducted brief expedition-type field visits and had very little knowledge of indigenous languages, as is evident from his own descriptions of ethnographic* research.

Ethnographers responded by turning their critical eye inward, upon their own preconceptions and social position and the larger power structures that privilege the wealthy and educated over their informants. The fact that anthropologists are their own research instruments and therefore cannot help but affect the field of observation and quality of the data has had positive effects on scholarship. On the other hand, it has cast doubt on the validity of previous ethnographic accounts and the comparative spirit of earlier scholars, including Mauss.

Mauss's ideas emerged during the formative phase of modern sociology* and consequently have influenced work across the humanities and social sciences. Mauss was an independent thinker but also a great collaborator who believed in intellectual reciprocity. It is fitting that his ideas did not give rise to specific schools of thought but rather have been influential in a variety of understated and at times indirect ways.

In Current Scholarship

The Gift continues to inspire scholarship, literature, and social and political debate, particularly among French writers. Mauss's (and Durkheim's) demonstration of the lack of an intrinsic connection between the properties of sacred*—spiritually important—objects and the meanings assigned to them converged, in time, with the influential Swiss linguist Ferdinand de Saussure's* teachings on language. This shared insight had far-reaching consequences for structuralist approaches to the study of language and myth led by Lévi-Strauss, and poststructuralist* work pioneered by the psychoanalyst Jacques Lacan* in psychology, linguistics, and literature;[6] poststructuralist theory rejected structuralist ideas, particularly the idea that it was possible to arrive at any objective truth in the course of analysis. The philosopher Paul Ricoeur's* concept of "the economy of the gift," among other ideas, drew directly from Mauss.[7] Other French scholars who have taken inspiration from Mauss's work on exchange and human relationships include the philosophers Jean-Luc Marion,* Maurice Godelier,* and Jacques Derrida* (a thinker noted for an approach to the analysis of symbol and meaning known as "deconstructionism").[8]

The Gift has also had a lasting impact on the sociology and anthropology* of economic and political systems, as in the German sociologist Helmuth Berking's* *Sociology of Giving*.[9] In part through the Hungarian American thinker Karl Polanyi's* influential work on the social history of Europe, Mauss's ideas reached a receptive audience of American scholars and supported their approach to and interest in economic anthropology.[10] Recent work in this area includes studies on the economics and cultural value of creativity in commercial society by the American writer Lewis Hyde;* the history of formal rules for gift-giving by the American writer and legal scholar Richard Hyland;* and gift exchange in the industrial era by the American historian Harry Liebersohn.*[11]

Finally, Mauss's call to combine political and scholarly writing has been taken up by scholars interested in contemporary social policy such as Alan Schrift.*[12] The anti-utilitarian "Mouvement Anti-Utilitariste dans les Sciences Sociales" (MAUSS), founded in 1981 by the French thinkers Alain Caillé* and Gérald Berthoud,* focuses on economic, ethical, and environmental crises including income insecurity, a topic Mauss touches upon in his conclusion to *The Gift*.[13] Caillé remains the editor of the anti-utilitarian journal *Revue du MAUSS*. The name in the title, an acronym for the *Mouvement*, honors Mauss's lasting influence on French sociology.

NOTES

1   Mary Douglas, "Foreword: No Free Gifts," in *The Gift* by Marcel Mauss (London: Routledge, 2000); Seth Leacock, "The Ethnological Theory of Marcel Mauss," *American Anthropologist* 56 (1954): 58–71.

2   Marcel Mauss, "Les Techniques du Corps," *Journal de Psychologie Normale et Pathologique* XXXII, nos 3–4 (1934): 271–93.

3   Pierre Bourdieu, *Outline of a Theory of Practice* (Cambridge: Cambridge University Press, 1977); Clifford Geertz, "From the Native's Point of View," in *Local Knowledge* by Clifford Geertz (New York: Basic Books, 1983), 54–70; Victor Turner, *Dramas, Fields, and Metaphors: Symbolic Action in Human Society* (Ithaca, NY: Cornell University Press, 1974); Victor Turner, *The Ritual Process: Structure and Anti-Stucture* (Chicago: Aldine, 1969).

4   Geertz, "From the Native's Point of View," 54–5.

5   Lise M. Dobrin and Ira Bashkow, "'Arapesh Warfare': Reo Fortune's
     Veiled Critique of Margaret Mead's Sex and Temperament," *American
     Anthropologist* 112, no. 3 (2010): 370–83; Margaret Mead, *Sex and
     Temperament in Three Primitive Societies* (New York: William Morrow, 1935).

6   Ferdinand De Saussure, *Course in General Linguistics* (New York: McGraw-
     Hill, 1959).

7   Paul Ricoeur, *History, Memory, Forgetting* (Chicago: University of Chicago
     Press, 2004).

8   Jean-Luc Marion, *Being Given: Toward a Phenomenology of Givenness* (Palo
     Alta, CA: Stanford University Press, 2002); Maurice Godelier, *L'Enigme du
     Don* (Paris: Fayard, 1996); Jacques Derrida, *The Gift of Death* (Chicago:
     University of Chicago Press, 2007); Jacques Derrida, *Given Time* (Chicago:
     University of Chicago Press, 1992).

9   Helmuth Berking, *Sociology of Giving* (London: Sage Publications, 1999).

10   Leacock, "The Ethnological Theory," 65; Karl Polanyi, *The Great
     Transformation: The Political and Economic Origins of Our Time* (New York:
     Farrar and Rinehart, 1944).

11   Lewis Hyde, *The Gift: Imagination and the Erotic Life of Property* (New York:
     Vintage Books, 2008); Richard Hyland, *Gifts: A Study in Comparative Law*
     (Oxford: Oxford University Press, 2009); H*arry Liebersohn,* The Return of
     the Gift: European History of a Global Idea (New York: Cambridge University
     Press, 2011).

12   Alan D. Schrift (ed.), *The Logic of the Gift: Toward an Ethic of Generosity*
     (London: Routledge, 1997).

13   Alain Caillé, *Anthropologie du Don: Le Tiers Paradigme* (Paris: Desclée de
     Brouwer, 2000).

MODULE 11
IMPACT AND INFLUENCE TODAY

KEY POINTS

- *The Gift* remains a foundational text in the teaching of anthropology.* The book continues to influence scholarly interpretations of reciprocal* exchange and its relationship to social cohesiveness, peace, and well-being.

- The text remains relevant to ongoing analysis of the political and economic implications of gifts and commercial transactions for societies and individuals.

- Today, scholars have filled gaps in knowledge of economic exchange across cultures, suggesting ways for individuals and societies to strengthen social relationships, improve well-being, and avoid interpersonal and international conflict.

Position

Marcel Mauss's *The Gift* was written at a time in which Western scholars, who lived in hierarchical societies themselves, took for granted the existence of rulers and social inequalities. Critical analysis of power, conflict, and internal divisions as taken up by the sociologist and philosopher Pierre Bourdieu,* came later. Today, the blind spots in Mauss's work have been filled by others, opening the door to new readings of his conclusions and their implications for economic policy and interpersonal relationships.

Mauss's unconscious application of a conceptual framework typical of his class, gender, and historical moment to populations across the globe is evident in his consideration of women as trade goods and men as universal decision-makers.[1] The inappropriateness of this perspective has been demonstrated by the US anthropologist Annette

> **❝ We should not take material acquisitiveness for granted. As Marcel Mauss put it, it is not something behind us, a natural condition, so much as it is before us, a moral value. Hence it is not so much an inevitability as an invention. ❞**
>
> Marshall Sahlins, *Apologies to Thucydides: Understanding History as Culture and Vice Versa*

Weiner* with regard to the Trobriand Islands and by the British anthropologist Marilyn Strathern* in relation to Melanesia.*2 The early anthropologists' blind spot is a testament to the power of unconscious assumptions to distort perceptions, for these early anthropologists overlooked glaring examples of gender interdependence and the far-reaching implications of matrilineal kinship (family relationships in the female line).

Mauss's uncritical acceptance of hierarchy is evident in his description of the transmission of both symbolic and institutional systems and inequalities through reciprocal exchange from generation to generation. He did not have the benefit of knowledge acquired decades later about classless, leaderless, gender-egalitarian societies that live by mobile gathering and hunting, or foraging.*3 Since the 1970s, around 50 such populations have been studied by anthropologists. These populations are the true champions of reciprocity. They are different from the rare form of sedentary (settled) foraging society represented by the populations of the Northwest Coast of the United States described in *The Gift*, which had leaders, social hierarchies, and stores of durable wealth.

Foraging societies practice a highly rule-based form of reciprocity, but they are also great defenders of individual autonomy (the capacity to act as an individual). Foraging populations challenge Mauss and Émile Durkheim's* assumption that individuality only emerges fully in complex modern societies. This does not make Mauss's work irrelevant. On the contrary, a revised view of reciprocity and redistribution extends the book's influence to current debates about political and economic issues and interpersonal relationships.

Interaction

Mobile foraging societies, which Marshall Sahlins* has famously called "the original affluent society," are small groups of individuals and families who live together without formal leaders.[4] They do not store food or accumulate more possessions than they can easily carry. Food is shared according to strict, elaborate rules, especially if it involves something rare. On average, women and men contribute about equal amounts of food. Foragers work fewer hours and enjoy better health than farmers.

Similarly to the villagers in Mauss's analysis, foragers benefit from reciprocity between groups because it protects against scarcity and prevents violent conflict. Within groups, reciprocity is a leveling device that keeps people humble and prevents feelings of envy. Arrogance is seen as a threat to individual autonomy and a menace that leads to violence. Failure to work or fulfill family and other obligations likewise is socially condemned.

Foraging societies present a challenge to Western assumptions about prehistory and consequently human nature. Taken-for-granted traits such as greed, hierarchy, male dominance, territoriality, aggressiveness, and stark self-interest all fall under the weight of evidence along with the harsh backdrop of short lives, constant misery, and servile submission to tyrants. This scenario is the core of utilitarian* philosophies of all kinds (that is, roughly, philosophies that equate usefulness and value), including the free-market economics that underpin today's system of capitalism* and today's version of social Darwinism[5] (the use of evolutionary theory to explain the different traits and fortunes of individuals or groups of people as a consequence of their biological inferiority or superiority), which incorporates the science of genetics.

The connection between reciprocity and reduced conflict described by Mauss has been confirmed by anthropologists who have studied the connection between warfare and intertribal marriages and other exchanges.[6] Other evidence comes from informal legal systems that bring together people in dispute in a community setting where whole families engage in reconciliation.[7] Cross-cultural exchanges create enduring relationships that help prevent international conflict. On the other hand, as Mauss has shown, gifts that cannot be returned, such as disaster relief and foreign aid, only increase the giver's status and power at the expense of the receiver's.[8]

The Continuing Debate

Mauss did not try to reconcile inequality with social solidarity.* Foraging societies show that inequality is not in the nature of things, supporting the anthropological project of exploring power and discord within societies. As we have seen, the absence of the accumulation of material goods together with enforced fairness in reciprocal exchange prevents the emergence of classes. Gender equality arises out of complementary or independent food gathering. However, the Hungarian American anthropologist Ernestine Friedl* has shown that egalitarianism suffers in the rare cases where men control the distribution of a scarce, unpredictable resource such as meat from large animals. Control over things with exchange value creates inequalities.[9] This pattern illustrates how reciprocal exchange can affect women and men differently within the same society. It also suggests that wherever one gender controls precious resources including honors and favors, there will be a higher level of inequality.

Friedl's analysis shares Mauss's premise that all reciprocal exchange is socially, economically, and politically meaningful. Exchange may involve non-monetary items or, alternatively, as in societies with money, the same resource may be used either for the benefit of the household (demonstrating what is termed "use value") or for cultivating potentially fruitful relationships outside the household ("exchange value"). Both reciprocal exchange and transactional sale-and-purchase coexist in all societies, as Mauss showed.

The implication is that solidarity is more likely to grow out of egalitarian systems of exchange, which preserve individual autonomy while maintaining social cohesion, than in situations of inequality. In this light, Mauss's priorities for the good society do not turn out be incompatible. Individuality and the obligation to work and defend one's own interests (from self to society) do not exclude society's obligations to return the gift (through education, income protection, fair prices for food and housing, fair wages for services, and protection of health and life). The key is a more comprehensive view of individualism, as Mauss's recommended steps against greed, accumulation, and unrestricted profit-taking demand changes to a legal framework that is based on a utilitarian vision of the individual. Current scholarship on the relationship between high levels of social integration and more favorable economic, health, education, and crime statistics lends further support to Mauss's vision in *The Gift*.[10]

NOTES

1   Marcel Mauss, *The Gift: The Form and Reason for Exchange in Archaic Societies* (London: Routledge, 1990), 5–6.

2   Marilyn Strathern, *The Gender of the Gift: Problems with Women and Problems with Society in Melanesia* (Berkeley: University of California Press, 1988); Annette Weiner, *Women of Value, Men of Renown: New Perspectives in Trobriand Exchange* (Austin: University of Texas Press, 1976).

3   Mauss mentions the "Pygmies" of Central Africa. They lived in forests near villagers and were known to missionaries and other foreigners long before most other groups of foragers.

4   Marshall Sahlins, *Stone Age Economics* (New York: Aldine de Gruyter, 1972), 1.

5   Marshall Sahlins, *The Western Illusion of Human Nature: With Reflections on the Long History of Hierarchy, Equality and the Sublimation of Anarchy in the West, and Comparative Notes on Other Conceptions of the Human Condition* (Chicago: Prickly Paradigm Press, 2008).

6   Douglas P. Fry, *The Human Potential for Peace: An Anthropological Challenge to Assumptions about War and Violence* (New York: Oxford University Press, 2006).

7   Fry, *The Human Potential*.

8   Lee Cronk, "Strings Attached," *The Sciences* 29, no. 3 (1988): 2–4.

9   Ernestine Friedl, "Society and Sex Roles," *Human Nature* 1 (1978): 8–75.

10   Marcel Mauss, *The Gift*, 68–89; Richard Wilkinson and Kate Pickett, *The Spirit Level: Why Greater Equality Makes Societies Stronger* (New York: Bloomsbury Press, 2009).

MODULE 12
WHERE NEXT?

KEY POINTS

- *The Gift* is a seminal text for its contributions to knowledge about the connection between gift cycles and social relationships, its participation in a trajectory of ideas, and its capacity to launch new ideas as times change.

- Mauss's work on the sacred* or magical elements of reciprocal* gift exchange is likely to extend the book's impact further into the future.

- Mauss's analysis of giving and receiving, including the transfer of mystical qualities, is relevant to scholarship on the trade in body organs and tissues, social relationships in the age of social media, and other concerns of current times.

Potential

The sacred elements of gift exchange explored by Marcel Mauss in *The Gift* point to many possibilities for further investigation. To illustrate, Mauss notes that in archaic societies* religious sacrifice is a means for people to maintain reciprocal obligations with the divine.[1] This involves gifts to the spirits as well as alms to the poor, in recognition of past favor and as an instrument through which to draw continued benefits. Research on the degree to which religious feeling motivates charitable giving in commercial societies is one avenue for Mauss's influence to be felt. His proposal that the rich be encouraged to see themselves as the temporary custodians of wealth obtained through some kind of supernatural favor, with corresponding duties as the financial guardians of others, has a place in contemporary debates about tax laws, charitable giving, and education and social services.

❝ Human organs are regularly subjected to elaborate metaphorical reworking that ultimately silences [ethical] unease. The most pervasive and obvious example involves relabeling organs as 'gifts of life,' a process that quickly mystifies the economic realities of their origins. **❞**

Lesley Sharp,* "Commodified Kin: Death, Mourning, and Competing Claims on the Bodies of Organ Donors in the United States"

These would need to address the contradiction, pointed out by Mauss, between giving as a spiritual obligation and the fact that sacred gift cycles support the social system as it stands.

Another path for Mauss's ideas is the role of magic in modern society. It has been pointed out that people in Western society continue to attribute supernatural power to things like special foods favored by ancient peoples, or spring water drawn from faraway places.[2] Popular concepts such as *karma* (the Buddhist and Hindu belief that accumulated merit determines one's fortune in this or subsequent lives) and "paying it forward" (performing positive actions as part of a cycle of good) suggest a perception that supernatural forces are at work in individual lives, that people are interconnected in mysterious ways, and that there can be distant consequences to one's daily actions. This is in spite of a return to utilitarianism* in economics and politics (a return to highly pragmatic assumptions and policies in which utility is favored over considerations that cannot be measured, such as ethics), and the veneration of science. The sacred or magical meaning alive in contemporary culture provides an enormous field for analysis inspired by Mauss's ideas.

Future Directions

Mauss's book suggests that a pure gift given out of generosity and without any expectation of a return is a logical impossibility, for there is always the potential for hidden nonmaterial benefits such as prestige or self-gratification. In relation to blood donation, Richard Titmuss,* the British founder of the academic discipline of social policy, allows that donors may experience social approval and feel that they might some day need a transfusion themselves, but argues that they consciously give blood as a moral act for the sake of social solidarity.*[3] To encourage donations, then, the gift must be isolated from the corrupting influence of money.

The medical anthropologist Margaret Lock* argues, however, that this separation derives from an artificial and unnecessarily stark distinction between market* and reciprocal exchange. She notes that when traditional economies become integrated into the market, they do not shed existing systems of reciprocal gift exchange but rather maintain a set of parallel or hybrid institutions.*[4] Likewise, in the donation industry, a framework for biological transfers based on transactions coexists with an unrecognized system of reciprocal exchange in which gifts carry social obligations.

Lock explains that the transplant industry purposely "fetishizes" organs in the sense used by the influential German economist and political philosopher Karl Marx:* they become objects of extraordinary value in a process Marx termed "commodity objectification," obscuring the exploitative relationships in production and consumption. Lock argues that organs are also fetishized in the original sense, recognized by Mauss, of being endowed with individuality and magical power: "Body parts remain infused with life and even personality … Once an organ is procured and transferred, the recipient is severely reprimanded, even thought of as exhibiting pathology, if he attributes this life-saving organ with animistic qualities."[5]

Medical staff take pains to define the gift as freely given, skirting ethical questions through the concept of the gift-as-object detached from all suffering as well as corporate interest. The system presents organs as literally disembodied commodities (roughly, useful objects) with no human content and no capacity to generate obligations—but donor and recipient families know otherwise and build relationships just the same.[6]

Summary

Mauss shows that gifts bind individuals, families, societies, and nations in a perpetual cycle of mutual indebtedness. Gifts are alive with personhood* and spiritual values. They demand to be repaid, one way or another. These ideas are highly relevant to contemporary society, useful for analyzing the economic and moral dimensions of voluntary biological transfers including, increasingly, DNA—the biological material in which genetic information is encoded and passed down.[7] Mauss's insights shed light on voluntary gifts of money for business development or personal needs through crowdfunding (the practice of raising money for small ventures through personal donations, especially via online communities), and knowledge through open source software, free content, and websites that serve as nodes for technical and creative exchanges.[8]

In addition, Mauss's analysis suggests how purely commercial transactions represent missed opportunities for building social solidarity. Gift cycles dictate a time lag that projects the relationship into the future; although this may be against the people's will, it brings them concrete benefits. Research has confirmed that greater social cohesiveness improves health and mental well-being, and that the extent of mutual obligations is connected to the degree of social solidarity. Mauss's desire to work out how individual autonomy can be reconciled with social embeddedness in mass society—that is, the ways in which economic behavior is constrained by society's non-economic institutions—has been fulfilled by studies on clubs and volunteer associations. In these subgroups of large industrialized societies, social cohesiveness arises out of mutual obligations and the active avoidance of hierarchy, and is favorable to individual well-being.[9]

Mauss has taught generations of readers that gifts are both expressive and instrumental. Exchanges between people—as individuals or as members of a group—take part within larger systems of rules, inequalities, and power. Whether they involve money, material goods, or purely intangible things, transfers carry culturally constructed symbolic values and meanings and strengthen social relationships.

NOTES

1   H. Hubert and M. Mauss, *Sacrifice: Its Nature and Functions* (Routledge: London, 1964).

2   Marshall Sahlins, *The Western Illusion of Human Nature: With Reflections on the Long History of Hierarchy, Equality and the Sublimation of Anarchy in the West, and Comparative Notes on Other Conceptions of the Human Condition* (Chicago: Prickly Paradigm Press, 2008).

3   Richard Titmuss, *The Gift Relationship: From Human Blood to Social Policy* (New York: New Press, 1997).

4   Margaret Lock, *Twice Dead: Organ Transplants and the Reinvention of Death* (Berkeley: University of California Press, 2001), 316.

5   Lock, *Twice Dead*, 320.

6   Lesley A. Sharp, "Commodified Kin: Death, Mourning, and Competing Claims on the Bodies of Organ Donors in the United States," *American Anthropologist* 103, no. 1 (2001): 112–33.

7   Deepa Reddy, "Good Gifts for a Common Good: Blood and Bioethics in the Market of Genetic Research," *Cultural Anthropology* 22, no. 3 (2007): 429–72.

8   Christopher Kelty, *Two Bits: The Cultural Significance of Free Software* (Durham, NC: Duke University Press, 2008).

9   Richard Wilkinson and Kate Pickett, *The Spirit Level: Why Greater Equality Makes Societies Stronger* (New York: Bloomsbury Press, 2009).

GLOSSARY

GLOSSARY OF TERMS

Affinity: the principle of "like attracts like" and the basis for "sympathetic magic," by which rituals such as rain dances imitate the thing desired.

Agency: the freedom and resources necessary for knowing and realizing one's own will.

Ancient Eurasia: ancient civilizations including Greek, Roman, Indian, and Middle Eastern societies.

Animism: a belief in spirits.

L'Année Sociologique: a journal established in 1898 by French social scientist Émile Durkheim to publish his own work and that of his students in the new discipline of sociology, which he had founded.

Anthropology: the study of the biological and cultural history and current variability of humankind.

Anti-Semitism: animosity, prejudice, and discrimination directed at Jews or Judaism.

Archaic societies: Mauss's term for contemporary indigenous societies as well as ancient civilizations representing a middle stage of social evolution.

Barter: the exchange of dissimilar items on the spot and possibly involving bargaining.

Bolshevism: the movement by which the Russian Social Democratic Workers' Party worked from 1903 to 1917 to seize power, establish a communist government, and within five years create the Union of Soviet Socialist Republics.

Capitalism: the economic and social model founded on the private ownership of industry and business that is dominant in the West (and increasingly throughout the Western world) today.

Clan: a group of relatives (whether by blood or marriage) whose kinship is based on the belief that they share a common ancestor.

Collective representations: shared beliefs and understandings.

Collectivism: ethical, political, and social philosophies focused on the group and opposed to individualism.

Communism: a political ideology that relies on state ownership of the means of production, the collectivization of labor, and the abolition of social class. It was the ideology of the Soviet Union (1917–91).

Comparative analysis: a comparison of societies or groups through their different social systems, artifacts, or features.

Contagion: the principle in "primitive" magic derived from belief in the permanent presence of mystical forces in things such as body products, which allows for manipulation of these forces through contact with the infused object.

Cooperative movement: a nineteenth-century European promotion of alternative economic institutions in response to social upheaval and labor insecurity associated with the Industrial Revolution and the mechanization of production.

Culture: a dynamic and unbounded set of beliefs, behavioral expectations, values, creative forms, and knowledge shared by a group of people.

Currency: any medium of exchange, from shells and agricultural products to gold and paper money.

Empirical approach: the idea that all knowledge should be gained by experience, by using experiments and observation to gather facts.

Eskimo: indigenous peoples of the Far North, including the Arctic coasts of North America, Greenland, and Siberia; also known as Inuit.

Ethnography: the systematic study of a group of people through long-term immersion and knowledge of the local language; also used to refer to a written analysis of data gathered through fieldwork.

Ethnology: the discipline concerned with analysis of ethnographic data and cross-cultural similarities and differences.

Foraging: a way of life based on food collection rather than cultivation or herding; also known as hunting and gathering.

French Workers' Party: a socialist political party in France formed in 1880 and merged into the French Socialist Party in 1905.

Habitus: in antiquity, the combination of constitutional and environmental forces that shapes individual physical existence and specific vulnerabilities to disease. In current academic usage, the concept emphasizes the embodiment of social and cultural conditions.

Hau: the Maori concept for the power of a certain class of gifts that compels people to pass them on and allow them to return to their place of origin.

Historical particularism: a theoretical movement in anthropology associated with Franz Boas that stresses the importance of recording details of group life in relation to historical context and attending to the uniqueness of individual societies.

Holistic: concerned with the whole and the interdependence of parts.

Indigenous peoples: the original inhabitants of a territory; often used in reference to people displaced or marginalized by governments or settlers from elsewhere.

Institut d'Ethnologie: the French ethnological institute founded in 1925 by Lucien Lévy-Bruhl, Marcel Mauss, and Paul Rivet.

Institution: a conventional relationship or activity such as marriage or retirement; also, a formal, legal entity such as a school or court of law.

Kinship: the bond between people that arises through birth, marriage, baptism, adoption, and other social means of defining relatedness.

Kula: a circular ceremonial exchange of armbands and necklaces in opposite directions from one island to another in the Trobriand Islands.

Liberalism: a political philosophy based on autonomous individualism, free market economics, and law-based governance free of interference in individual liberties.

Mana: the Polynesian and Melanesian concept of a pervasive spiritual force that permeates the universe, can attach to objects, and reveals itself through some people's advantages and powers.

Maori: the indigenous people of New Zealand.

Market economy: the economic exchange of goods based on established calculated values, not limited to exchange in actual physical markets.

Melanesia: the group of islands in the southwestern Pacific Ocean between the equator and northeast Australia, including the Solomon Islands, New Caledonia, and Papua New Guinea.

Personhood: the state of being an individual within a particular cultural and social context. In Western thought a "person" is a social individual while "selfhood" refers to the individual's internal experience.

Polynesia: the scattered islands in the south-central Pacific Ocean situated between New Zealand, Hawaii, and Easter Island.

Poststructuralism: A variety of theoretical and methodological approaches that reject the principle of binary oppositions central to structuralism and emphasize fluidity and change in conceptual categories and their meanings.

Potlatch: a ceremonial feast practiced by Native American populations in Northwest North America that includes gifts to the guests; between rival groups, a means for the competitive display of wealth and prestige through quantitatively increasing gifts and even the destruction of wealth objects.

Pygmies: indigenous peoples of the Central African forests.

Rationality: in economics, a characteristic of reasoning through which marginal costs and benefits are weighed in order to maximize utility.

Reciprocity: the cyclic exchange of material and intangible gifts and services between individuals or groups.

Revolutionary Socialist Workers' Party: a moderate reformers' party in France from 1890 to 1901 that promoted education and labor safeguards.

Sacred: a category and adjective referring to the sphere of ideas, rituals, and objects worthy of religious veneration.

Seasonality: changes in people's patterns of behavior according to the season of the year.

Social evolutionism: the belief that societies progress through a fixed series of stages of ever-increasing technological, social, and intellectual perfection; and that differences in the speed of evolution account for the coexistence of variably advanced societies.

Socialism: a political system in which the means of production (the tools and resources required by business and industry) are held in common ownership.

Sociology: the study of social behavior, social institutions, and the origins and organization of human society.

Solidarity: the degree of connectedness people feel for one another.

Soviet Union: the Union of Soviet Socialist Republics (USSR), a Eurasian empire that arose from the Russian Revolution in 1917 and consisted of Russia and 14 satellite states in Eastern Europe, the Baltic and Black Seas, and Central Asia, existing from 1922 to 1991.

Structural-functionalism: a theoretical approach in anthropology and sociology associated with A. R. Radcliffe-Brown and Bronislaw Malinowski that focuses on the ways in which societies are structured and the internal parts are integrated with one another.

Structuralism: an approach to the analysis of social, textual, or linguistic forms that involves arranging elemental components into a system of binary opposition; associated in anthropology with Claude Lévi-Strauss.

Totem: a neutral object that is infused with sacredness; the object through which a group of people symbolizes itself.

Trade: the formalized exchange of unalike items according to prescribed standards of value.

Tribes: a category of societies that are politically organized around kinship relations.

Utilitarianism: the idea that usefulness determines the value of things; eighteenth- and nineteenth-century English philosophical tradition associated with Jeremy Bentham and John Stuart Mill based on the ethical goal of maximizing utility for the collective, defined as the surfeit of well-being that remains after correcting for suffering (concisely, the greatest good for the greatest number of people).

Utility: in economics, the material and/or psychological usefulness to an individual consumer of purchased goods and services.

World War I: the war fought between 1914 and 1918 in which Austria-Hungary, Germany, Turkey, and Bulgaria were defeated by Great Britain, France, Italy, Russia, Japan, the United States, and other allies.

World War II: a global conflict from 1939 to 1945 that involved the world's great powers and numerous other countries around the globe. Fought between the Allies (the United States, Britain, France, the Soviet Union, and others) and the Axis powers (Germany, Italy, Japan, and others), it was seen as a major moral struggle between freedom and tyranny.

PEOPLE MENTIONED IN THE TEXT

Fredrik Barth (b. 1928) is a Norwegian anthropologist with a wide range of fieldwork experience. He is known for works on political and economic organization, ethnicity, and knowledge.

Georges Bataille (1897–1962) was a French writer and philosopher whose work spanned the humanistic disciplines and included transgressive novels and short stories.

Henri Beauchat (1878–1914) was a French sociologist and colleague of Durkheim and Mauss. He died of exposure and starvation on an island off the northeastern coast of Siberia along with other members of an expedition.

Ruth Benedict (1887–1948) was an American anthropologist interested in folklore, art, language, and personality. She is known for her comparative study of cultures and insights into the performative aspects of culture.

Jeremy Bentham (1748–1832) was a British jurist and philosopher, and founder of philosophical utilitarianism.

Helmuth Berking (b. c. 1952) is a German sociologist interested in economic and urban anthropology, social theory, and cultural identity.

Gérald Berthoud (b. 1935) is a Swiss sociologist and economist and cofounder with Alain Caillé of the Anti-Utilitarian Movement in the Social Sciences.

Maurice Bloch (b. 1939) is a British anthropologist who has carried out fieldwork in Madagascar. He is a distinguished academic and was a professor at the London School of Economics from 1983 onward.

Franz Boas (1858–1942) was a German American anthropologist associated with historical particularism in American anthropology and the study of Native Americans of the Northwest Coast. He is considered the "father of American anthropology."

Pierre Bourdieu (1930–2002) was a French sociologist, philosopher, and anthropologist interested in reflexivity, language, and the social sources and dynamics of power. He is known for concepts such as habitus and social, symbolic, and cultural capital.

Alain Caillé (b. 1944) is a French sociologist and economist, cofounder of the Anti-Utilitarian Movement in the Social Sciences, editor of the journal *MAUSS*, and author of numerous books inspired by *The Gift*.

Roger Caillois (1913–78) was a French writer, sociologist, and political philosopher. He is known for his work on the sacred, games and play, and Latin American literature.

Georges Condominas (1921–2011) was a French anthropologist who conducted research in Vietnam and was taught by Denise Paulme, Marcel Griaule, and Maurice Leenhardt.

Charles Darwin (1809–82) was a British naturalist, most famous for his work on evolutionary theory, and specifically for developing the theory of natural selection, the belief that all animals are descended from a common ancestor.

Jacques Derrida (1930–2004) was a French sociologist born in Algeria who pioneered a strain of symbolic analysis known as deconstruction.

Georges Devereux (1908–85) was a Hungarian French anthropologist and psychoanalyst, and close associate of Claude Lévi-Strauss. He is considered the father of ethnopsychiatry.

Mary Douglas (1921–2007) was a British social anthropologist interested in symbolism, comparative religion, and economic and environmental anthropology. She is best known for her structuralist analysis of sacred categories, *Purity and Danger* (1966).

Alfred Dreyfus (1859–1935) was a French artillery officer of Jewish background who in 1895 was sentenced by secret court martial to life imprisonment in exile for treason. A scandal over the "Dreyfus Affair" led to his receiving a presidential pardon in 1899. In 1906, Dreyfus was officially exonerated by the military and returned to service.

Émile Durkheim (1858–1917) was a French social scientist considered the founder of sociology. Durkheim's sociology fuses Comte's positivist sociology with a humanistic focus on shared beliefs and values. He is best known for his writings on alienation, suicide, and sociological methods.

Alfred Victor Espinas (1844–1922) was a French philosopher who wrote about political philosophy, intellectual history, and the evolution of human thought.

Edward Evan Evans-Pritchard (1902–73) was one of the founders of British social anthropology and a follower of Radcliffe-Brown's structural-functionalism. He is known for studies on the Azande and Nuer in South Sudan.

Paul Fauconnet (1874–1938) was a French sociologist and member of the original group formed around the journal *L'Année Sociologique*.

Raymond Firth (1901–2002) was an anthropologist from New Zealand who taught for many decades at the London School of Economics and disputed Marcel Mauss's interpretation of certain Maori beliefs discussed in *The Gift*.

James George Frazer (1854–1941) was a Scottish sociologist and anthropologist who compiled 12 volumes of religious beliefs from around the world, organized according to his belief that human thought progressed from magic to religion to science. *The Golden Bough* was published in three editions in 1890, 1900, and 1906–15.

Ernestine Friedl (b. 1920) is a Hungarian-born American anthropologist with interests in gender, rural Greece, and the Chippewa of Wisconsin. She is known for a seminal article on "Society and Sex Roles."

Clifford Geertz (1926–2006) was an American anthropologist who conducted fieldwork in Indonesia. Together with Victor Turner, he is considered the founder of symbolic and interpretive anthropology.

Maurice Godelier (b. 1934) is a French philosopher and anthropologist who conducted fieldwork in Papua New Guinea. He is known for his contributions to economic and development anthropology and the analysis of inequality, gender, and power.

Walter Goldschmidt (1903–2010) was an American anthropologist with a wide range of fieldwork experience and interests. He is known for his analysis of the implications of industrial versus small, independent farming for local communities in California.

Octave Hamelin (1856–1907) was a French philosopher at the University of Bordeaux who was a close associate of Durkheim's.

Robert Hertz (1881–1915) was a French sociologist of religion and close colleague of Durkheim and Mauss. He was killed in World War I.

Henri Hubert (1872–1927) was a French historian and sociologist interested in religion who collaborated closely with Mauss on essays and book reviews.

Lewis Hyde (b. 1945) is an American writer, critic, and translator. He is known for his work on creativity and commerce.

Richard Hyland (b. 1949) is an American writer and legal scholar. He is known for his comparative and historical analysis of informal and formal laws concerning gift-giving.

Jacques Lacan (1901–81) was a French psychoanalyst and scholar of sociology, literary theory, and linguistics. He was the intellectual center of poststructuralism.

Maurice Leenhardt (1878–1954) was a French clergyman and anthropologist who conducted fieldwork in New Caledonia. He was a follower of Mauss's teachings on methodology, and is considered the founder of Melanesian anthropology.

Claude Lévi-Strauss (1908–2009) was a French sociologist born in Belgium and the "father of structuralism."

Henri Lévy-Bruhl (1884–1964) was a French sociologist trained by Mauss who was interested in comparative law, religion, and modes of thought.

Lucien Lévy-Bruhl (1857–1939) was a French philosopher and sociologist interested in the evolution of the mind. Together with Mauss and Paul Rivet, he helped found the Institut d'Ethnologie in Paris.

Harry Liebersohn (b. 1951) is an American historian who is interested in intellectual history, social theory, travel writing, religion, creativity, and gift exchange.

Margaret Lock (b. 1936) is a British-born Canadian anthropologist specializing in medical anthropology. She is known for her work on aging, organ transplants, and comparative medical knowledge and practices.

Bronislaw Malinowski (1884–1942) was a Polish anthropologist, sociologist, and ethnographer who is considered the cofounder (with A. R. Radcliffe-Brown) of British social anthropology. He is best known for his work on the *kula* gift exchange system in the Trobriand Islands.

Jean-Luc Marion (b. 1946) is a French philosopher known for his work on religion, love, and giving.

Karl Marx (1818–83) was a highly influential economist and social theorist; Marxist theory, a method of social and historical analysis that emphasizes the struggle between the classes, among other things, is derived from his works, notably *Capital* (1867–94) and *The Communist Manifesto* (1848).

Margaret Mead (1901–78) was an American anthropologist and public figure who conducted research in Melanesia and the South Pacific on gender roles, sexuality, childrearing, and adolescence.

John Stuart Mill (1806–73) was a British civil servant and political and economic philosopher who believed that individual economic initiative and responsibility were the basis of liberty.

Lewis Henry Morgan (1818–81) was an American lawyer, politician, and anthropologist who studied kinship, social structure, and customs according to the belief that societies progressed from savagery to barbarism to civilization.

Denise Paulme (1909–98) was one of the first academically trained female French anthropologists. She was one of Mauss's students and studied literature, ritual, and social and political organization in African societies beginning in the 1930s.

Karl Polanyi (1886–1964) was a Hungarian American philosopher, anthropologist, social historian, and political-economist. He was the originator of the sociocultural approach to economics known as substantivism and is best known for his 1944 book, *The Great Transformation*.

Alfred Reginald Radcliffe-Brown (1881–1955) was a British philosopher, psychologist, and anthropologist known as the "father of British structural-functionalism." Together with Bronislaw Malinowski, he is considered the founder of British social anthropology.

Paul Ricoeur (1913–2005) was a French philosopher interested in history, psychology, identity, language, literary criticism, and theological studies. His work on Christian theology was influenced by Mauss's analysis of reciprocal exchange.

Paul Rivet (1876–1958) was a French physician and ethnographer who conducted research in South America. Together with Mauss and Lucien Lévy-Bruhl, he helped found the Institut d'Ethnologie in Paris.

Jean Rouch (1917–2004) was a French anthropologist and filmmaker who worked for decades in Africa and is known for his technique of blending documentary and fictional elements in film.

Marshall Sahlins (b. 1930) is an American anthropologist who conducted fieldwork in the Pacific and has made significant contributions to anthropological theory. He is a professor emeritus of anthropology and social sciences at the University of Chicago.

Ferdinand de Saussure (1857–1913) was a Swiss linguist who is considered a founding father of modern linguistics and the study of meaning-making or signification. He is best known for his posthumously published lectures on linguistics.

Alan Schrift (b. 1955) is an American philosopher who is interested in nineteenth- and twentieth-century philosophy and the theme of generosity and giving.

Lesley Sharp (b. 1956) is an American medical anthropologist who has done fieldwork in Madagascar. She is known for her work on body commodification and the social construction of the self.

Georg Simmel (1858–1918) was a German philosopher and sociologist, and author of a seminal work on economic systems as social and cultural systems, *The Philosophy of Money*.

Herbert Spencer (1820–1903) was a British philosopher who advanced a comprehensive evolutionary theory by which species, nature, society, and the human mind progressed from simple to complex forms.

Marilyn Strathern (b. 1941) is a British anthropologist who has conducted fieldwork in Papua New Guinea. She is known for her work on gender, kinship, and reproduction, which has challenged earlier anthropologists' interpretations of exchange in Melanesia.

Richard Titmuss (1907–73) was a self-taught British scholar who founded the academic discipline of social policy in England. He is known for his work on giving and altruism in relation to social and health policy.

Alexis de Tocqueville (1805–59) was a French historian and political theorist. He is best known for his analysis of political economy and social conditions in the United States, *Democracy in America* (1835 and 1840).

Victor Turner (1920–83) was a Scottish social anthropologist known for his work in Africa on rites of passage, ritual, and symbols. Together with Clifford Geertz, he is considered the founder of symbolic and interpretive anthropology.

Edward Burnett Tylor (1832–1917) was a British anthropologist who advanced a social evolutionary approach to the study of cultures. He is considered one of the founders of academic anthropology.

Thorstein Veblen (1857–1929) was an American sociologist and economist who developed the concept of conspicuous consumption to describe competitive spending behavior. He wrote *The Theory of the Leisure Class* (1899).

Max Weber (1864–1920) was a German scholar with Marcel Mauss's same interests and expertise in law, philosophy, economics, and sociology. He is best known for *The Protestant Ethic and the Spirit of Capitalism*.

Annette Weiner (1933–97) was an American anthropologist who conducted fieldwork in the Trobriand Islands a half-century after Malinowski. She is known for her work on the social and political roles of women in relation to reciprocal exchange systems.

Émile Zola (1840–1902) was a French novelist and playwright who promoted naturalism in fiction. He is known for his 1898 letter, "J'Accuse," in defense of the falsely accused French army officer Alfred Dreyfus.

WORKS CITED

WORKS CITED

Barth, Fredrik, Robert Parkin, Andre Gingrich, and Sydel Silverman. *One Discipline, Four Ways: British, German, French, and American Anthropology*. Chicago: University of Chicago Press, 2005.

Benedict, Ruth. *Patterns of Culture*. New York: Houghton Mifflin, 2005.

Berking, Helmuth. *Sociology of Giving: Theory, Culture, and Society*. Translated by Patrick Camiller. London: Sage Publications, 1999.

Boas, Franz. "The Limitations of the Comparative Method of Anthropology." *Science* 4, no. 103 (1896): 901–8.

"Changes in Bodily Form of Descendants of Immigrants." *American Anthropologist* 14, no. 3 (1912): 530–62.

Race, Language, and Culture. London: Collier-Macmillan, 1940.

Kwakiutl Ethnography. Chicago: University of Chicago Press, 1966.

Bohannan, Paul, and Mark Glazer (eds). *High Points in Anthropology*. New York: Alfred A. Knopf, 1988.

Bourdieu, Pierre. *Outline of a Theory of Practice*. Cambridge: Cambridge University Press, 1977.

Caillé, Alain. *Anthropologie du Don: Le Tiers Paradigme*. Paris: Desclée de Brouwer, 2000.

Condominas, Georges. "Marcel Mauss, Père de l'ethnographie française." *Critique* 28, no. 297 (1972): 118–39.

Cronk, Lee. "Strings Attached." *The Sciences* 29, no. 3 (1988): 2–4.

Derrida, Jacques. *Given Time*. Chicago: University of Chicago Press, 1992.

The Gift of Death. Chicago: University of Chicago Press, 2007.

Dobrin, Lise M., and Ira Bashkow. "'Arapesh Warfare': Reo Fortune's Veiled Critique of Margaret Mead's *Sex and Temperament*." *American Anthropologist* 112, no. 3 (2010): 370–83.

Douglas, Mary. "Foreword: No Free Gifts." In *The Gift*, by Marcel Mauss. London: Routledge, 2000.

Durkheim, Émile. *The Elementary Forms of the Religious Life*. New York: Free Press, 1915.

The Division of Labor in Society. New York: Free Press, 1984.

On Suicide. London: Penguin Books, 2006.

Durkheim, Émile, and Marcel Mauss. *Primitive Classification*. Chicago: University of Chicago Press, 1963.

Evans-Pritchard, E. E. *The Nuer: A Description of the Modes of Livelihood and Political Institutions of a Nilotic People*. Oxford: Clarendon Press, 1940.

Fauconnet, Paul, and Marcel Mauss. "Sociologie: Objet et Méthode." *La Grande Encyclopédie* 30 (1901): 165–76.

Firth, Raymond. *Primitive Economics of the New Zealand Maori*. London: Routledge, 1929.

Fournier, Marcel. *Marcel Mauss: A Biography*. Princeton, NJ: Princeton University Press, 2005.

Frazer, James George. *The Illustrated Golden Bough: A Study in Magic and Religion*. New York: Simon and Schuster, 1996.

Friedl, Ernestine. "Society and Sex Roles." *Human Nature* 1 (1978): 8–75.

Fry, Douglas P. *The Human Potential for Peace: An Anthropological Challenge to Assumptions about War and Violence*. New York: Oxford University Press, 2006.

Geertz, Clifford. "From the Native's Point of View." In *Local Knowledge*, by Clifford Geertz, 54–70. New York: Basic Books, 1983.

Godbout, Jacques, and Alain Caillé. *L'Esprit du Don*. Montréal and Paris: Éditions La Découverte, 1992.

Godelier, Maurice. *L'Enigme du Don*. Paris: Fayard, 1996.

Goldschmidt, Walter. "Untitled Review of *The Gift* by Marcel Mauss." *American Anthropologist* 57, no. 6 (1955): 1299–1300.

Hubert, Henri, and Marcel Mauss. *Sacrifice: its Nature and Functions*. Routledge: London, 1964.

Hyde, Lewis. *The Gift: Imagination and the Erotic Life of Property*. New York: Vintage Books, 2008.

Hyland, Richard. *Gifts: A Study in Comparative Law*. Oxford: Oxford University Press, 2009.

Kelty, Christopher. *Two Bits: The Cultural Significance of Free Software*. Durham, NC: Duke University Press, 2008.

Leacock, Seth. "The Ethnological Theory of Marcel Mauss." *American Anthropologist* 56 (1954): 58–71.

Lévi-Strauss, Claude. *The Elementary Structures of Kinship*. Boston: Beacon Press, 1969.

Introduction to the Work of Marcel Mauss. London: Routledge and Kegan Paul, 1987.

Liebersohn, Harry. *The Return of the Gift: European History of a Global Idea*. New York: Cambridge University Press, 2011.

Lock, Margaret. *Twice Dead: Organ Transplants and the Reinvention of Death*. Berkeley: University of California Press, 2001.

Malinowski, Bronislaw. *Argonauts of the Western Pacific: An Account of Native Enterprise and Adventure in the Archipelagos of Melanesian New Guinea*. London: Routledge, 1922.

Marion, Jean-Luc. *Being Given: Toward a Phenomenology of Givenness*. Palo Alta, CA: Stanford University Press, 2002.

Mauss, Marcel. "L'Enseignement de l'Histoire des Religions des Peuples Non-Civilisés à l'École des Hautes Études." *Revue de l'Histoire des Religions* 45 (1902): 36–55.

"Essai sur le Don: Forme et Raison de l'Échange dans les Sociétés Archaïques." *Année Sociologique* no. 1 (1923–4): 30–186.

"Effet Physique chez l'Individu de l'Idée de Mort Suggérée par la Collectivité." *Journal de Psychologie Normale et Pathologique* XXIII, no. 6 (1926): 653–69.

"Les Techniques du Corps." *Journal de Psychologie Normale et Pathologique* XXXII, nos 3–4 (1934): 271–93.

"Une Catégorie de l'Esprit Humain: La Notion de Personne, celle de 'Moi.'" *Journal of the Royal Anthropological Institute* XLVIII, no. 2 (1938): 263–81.

Manuel d'Ethnographie. Paris: Payot, 1947.

Sociologie et Anthropologie. Paris: Presses Universaires de France, 1950.

The Gift: Forms and Functions of Exchange in Archaic Societies. Glencoe, IL: Free Press, 1954.

"L'Oeuvre de Mauss par Lui-Même." *Revue Française de Sociologie* 20, nos 20–1 (1979).

The Gift: The Form and Reason for Exchange in Archaic Societies. London: Routledge, 1990.

The Gift: Expanded Edition. Chicago: University of Chicago Press for HAU, 2015.

Mauss, Marcel, and Henri Beauchat. *Seasonal Variation of the Eskimo: A Study in Social Morphology*. London: Routledge, 1979 (1906).

Mauss, Marcel, and Henri Hubert. "Essai sur la Nature et la Fonction du Sacrifice." *L'Année Sociologique* (1897–8): 29–138.

A General Theory of Magic. London: Routledge, 2001.

Mead, Margaret. *Sex and Temperament in Three Primitive Societies*. New York: William Morrow, 1935.

Morgan, Lewis Henry. *Ancient Society: Researches into the Lines of Human Progress from Savagery through Barbarism to Civilization*. New York: Henry Holt and Company, 1877.

Polanyi, Karl. *The Great Transformation: The Political and Economic Origins of Our Time*. New York: Farrar and Rinehart, 1944.

Radcliffe-Brown, Alfred Reginald. "Three Tribes of Western Australia." *Journal of the Royal Anthropological Institute* XLIII (1913).

The Andaman Islanders. Cambridge: Cambridge University Press, 1933.

Reddy, Deepa. "Good Gifts for a Common Good: Blood and Bioethics in the Market of Genetic Research." *Cultural Anthropology* 22, no. 3 (2007): 429–72.

Ricoeur, Paul. *History, Memory, Forgetting*. Chicago: University of Chicago Press, 2004.

Sahlins, Marshall. *Stone Age Economics*. New York: Aldine de Gruyter, 1972.

Apologies to Thucydides: Understanding History as Culture and Vice Versa. Chicago: University of Chicago Press, 2004.

The Western Illusion of Human Nature: With Reflections on the Long History of Hierarchy, Equality and the Sublimation of Anarchy in the West, and Comparative Notes on Other Conceptions of the Human Condition. Chicago: Prickly Paradigm Press, 2008.

De Saussure, Ferdinand. *Course in General Linguistics*. Translated by Wade Baskin. New York: McGraw-Hill, 1959.

Schrift, Alan D. (ed.). *The Logic of the Gift: Toward an Ethic of Generosity*. London: Routledge, 1997.

Sharp, Lesley A. "Commodified Kin: Death, Mourning, and Competing Claims on the Bodies of Organ Donors in the United States." *American Anthropologist* 103, no. 1 (2001): 112–33.

Simmel, Georg. *The Philosophy of Money*. London: Routledge, 1978.

Strathern, Marilyn. *The Gender of the Gift: Problems with Women and Problems with Society in Melanesia*. Berkeley: University of California Press, 1988.

Titmuss, Richard. *The Gift Relationship: From Human Blood to Social Policy*. New York: New Press, 1997.

Turner, Victor. *The Ritual Process: Structure and Anti-Structure*. Chicago: Aldine, 1969.

Dramas, Fields, and Metaphors: Symbolic Action in Human Society. Ithaca, NY: Cornell University Press, 1974.

Tylor, Edward Burnett. *Primitive Culture: Researches into the Development of Mythology, Philosophy, Religion, Art, and Custom*. London: J. Murray, 1871.

Veblen, Thorstein. *The Theory of the Leisure Class: An Economic Study of the Evolution of Institutions*. New York: MacMillan, 1899.

The Theory of the Leisure Class. Oxford: Oxford University Press, 2009.

Weber, Max. *The Protestant Ethic and the Spirit of Capitalism: The Relationships between Religion and the Economic and Social Life in Modern Culture.* Translated by Talcott Parsons. New York: Charles Scribner's Sons, 1958.

Weiner, Annette. *Women of Value, Men of Renown: New Perspectives in Trobriand Exchange*. Austin: University of Texas Press, 1976.

Wilkinson, Richard, and Kate Pickett. *The Spirit Level: Why Greater Equality Makes Societies Stronger*. New York: Bloomsbury Press, 2009.

THE MACAT LIBRARY
BY DISCIPLINE

AFRICANA STUDIES

Chinua Achebe's *An Image of Africa: Racism in Conrad's Heart of Darkness*
W. E. B. Du Bois's *The Souls of Black Folk*
Zora Neale Huston's *Characteristics of Negro Expression*
Martin Luther King Jr's *Why We Can't Wait*
Toni Morrison's *Playing in the Dark: Whiteness in the American Literary Imagination*

ANTHROPOLOGY

Arjun Appadurai's *Modernity at Large: Cultural Dimensions of Globalisation*
Philippe Ariès's *Centuries of Childhood*
Franz Boas's *Race, Language and Culture*
Kim Chan & Renée Mauborgne's *Blue Ocean Strategy*
Jared Diamond's *Guns, Germs & Steel: the Fate of Human Societies*
Jared Diamond's *Collapse: How Societies Choose to Fail or Survive*
E. E. Evans-Pritchard's *Witchcraft, Oracles and Magic Among the Azande*
James Ferguson's *The Anti-Politics Machine*
Clifford Geertz's *The Interpretation of Cultures*
David Graeber's *Debt: the First 5000 Years*
Karen Ho's *Liquidated: An Ethnography of Wall Street*
Geert Hofstede's *Culture's Consequences: Comparing Values, Behaviors, Institutes and Organizations across Nations*
Claude Lévi-Strauss's *Structural Anthropology*
Jay Macleod's *Ain't No Makin' It: Aspirations and Attainment in a Low-Income Neighborhood*
Saba Mahmood's *The Politics of Piety: The Islamic Revival and the Feminist Subjec*t
Marcel Mauss's *The Gift*

BUSINESS

Jean Lave & Etienne Wenger's *Situated Learning*
Theodore Levitt's *Marketing Myopia*
Burton G. Malkiel's *A Random Walk Down Wall Street*
Douglas McGregor's *The Human Side of Enterprise*
Michael Porter's *Competitive Strategy: Creating and Sustaining Superior Performance*
John Kotter's *Leading Change*
C. K. Prahalad & Gary Hamel's *The Core Competence of the Corporation*

CRIMINOLOGY

Michelle Alexander's *The New Jim Crow: Mass Incarceration in the Age of Colorblindness*
Michael R. Gottfredson & Travis Hirschi's *A General Theory of Crime*
Richard Herrnstein & Charles A. Murray's *The Bell Curve: Intelligence and Class Structure in American Life*
Elizabeth Loftus's *Eyewitness Testimony*
Jay Macleod's *Ain't No Makin' It: Aspirations and Attainment in a Low-Income Neighborhood*
Philip Zimbardo's *The Lucifer Effect*

ECONOMICS

Janet Abu-Lughod's *Before European Hegemony*
Ha-Joon Chang's *Kicking Away the Ladder*
David Brion Davis's *The Problem of Slavery in the Age of Revolution*
Milton Friedman's *The Role of Monetary Policy*
Milton Friedman's *Capitalism and Freedom*
David Graeber's *Debt: the First 5000 Years*
Friedrich Hayek's *The Road to Serfdom*
Karen Ho's *Liquidated: An Ethnography of Wall Street*

The Macat Library By Discipline

John Maynard Keynes's *The General Theory of Employment, Interest and Money*
Charles P. Kindleberger's *Manias, Panics and Crashes*
Robert Lucas's *Why Doesn't Capital Flow from Rich to Poor Countries?*
Burton G. Malkiel's *A Random Walk Down Wall Street*
Thomas Robert Malthus's *An Essay on the Principle of Population*
Karl Marx's *Capital*
Thomas Piketty's *Capital in the Twenty-First Century*
Amartya Sen's *Development as Freedom*
Adam Smith's *The Wealth of Nations*
Nassim Nicholas Taleb's *The Black Swan: The Impact of the Highly Improbable*
Amos Tversky's & Daniel Kahneman's *Judgment under Uncertainty: Heuristics and Biases*
Mahbub Ul Haq's *Reflections on Human Development*
Max Weber's *The Protestant Ethic and the Spirit of Capitalism*

FEMINISM AND GENDER STUDIES

Judith Butler's *Gender Trouble*
Simone De Beauvoir's *The Second Sex*
Michel Foucault's *History of Sexuality*
Betty Friedan's *The Feminine Mystique*
Saba Mahmood's *The Politics of Piety: The Islamic Revival and the Feminist Subject*
Joan Wallach Scott's *Gender and the Politics of History*
Mary Wollstonecraft's *A Vindication of the Rights of Woman*
Virginia Woolf's *A Room of One's Own*

GEOGRAPHY

The Brundtland Report's *Our Common Future*
Rachel Carson's *Silent Spring*
Charles Darwin's *On the Origin of Species*
James Ferguson's *The Anti-Politics Machine*
Jane Jacobs's *The Death and Life of Great American Cities*
James Lovelock's *Gaia: A New Look at Life on Earth*
Amartya Sen's *Development as Freedom*
Mathis Wackernagel & William Rees's *Our Ecological Footprint*

HISTORY

Janet Abu-Lughod's *Before European Hegemony*
Benedict Anderson's *Imagined Communities*
Bernard Bailyn's *The Ideological Origins of the American Revolution*
Hanna Batatu's *The Old Social Classes And The Revolutionary Movements Of Iraq*
Christopher Browning's *Ordinary Men: Reserve Police Batallion 101 and the Final Solution in Poland*
Edmund Burke's *Reflections on the Revolution in France*
William Cronon's *Nature's Metropolis: Chicago And The Great West*
Alfred W. Crosby's *The Columbian Exchange*
Hamid Dabashi's *Iran: A People Interrupted*
David Brion Davis's *The Problem of Slavery in the Age of Revolution*
Nathalie Zemon Davis's *The Return of Martin Guerre*
Jared Diamond's *Guns, Germs & Steel: the Fate of Human Societies*
Frank Dikotter's *Mao's Great Famine*
John W Dower's *War Without Mercy: Race And Power In The Pacific War*
W. E. B. Du Bois's *The Souls of Black Folk*
Richard J. Evans's *In Defence of History*
Lucien Febvre's *The Problem of Unbelief in the 16th Century*
Sheila Fitzpatrick's *Everyday Stalinism*

Eric Foner's *Reconstruction: America's Unfinished Revolution, 1863-1877*
Michel Foucault's *Discipline and Punish*
Michel Foucault's *History of Sexuality*
Francis Fukuyama's *The End of History and the Last Man*
John Lewis Gaddis's *We Now Know: Rethinking Cold War History*
Ernest Gellner's *Nations and Nationalism*
Eugene Genovese's *Roll, Jordan, Roll: The World the Slaves Made*
Carlo Ginzburg's *The Night Battles*
Daniel Goldhagen's *Hitler's Willing Executioners*
Jack Goldstone's *Revolution and Rebellion in the Early Modern World*
Antonio Gramsci's *The Prison Notebooks*
Alexander Hamilton, John Jay & James Madison's *The Federalist Papers*
Christopher Hill's *The World Turned Upside Down*
Carole Hillenbrand's *The Crusades: Islamic Perspectives*
Thomas Hobbes's *Leviathan*
Eric Hobsbawm's *The Age Of Revolution*
John A. Hobson's *Imperialism: A Study*
Albert Hourani's *History of the Arab Peoples*
Samuel P. Huntington's *The Clash of Civilizations and the Remaking of World Order*
C. L. R. James's *The Black Jacobins*
Tony Judt's *Postwar: A History of Europe Since 1945*
Ernst Kantorowicz's *The King's Two Bodies: A Study in Medieval Political Theology*
Paul Kennedy's *The Rise and Fall of the Great Powers*
Ian Kershaw's *The "Hitler Myth": Image and Reality in the Third Reich*
John Maynard Keynes's *The General Theory of Employment, Interest and Money*
Charles P. Kindleberger's *Manias, Panics and Crashes*
Martin Luther King Jr's *Why We Can't Wait*
Henry Kissinger's *World Order: Reflections on the Character of Nations and the Course of History*
Thomas Kuhn's *The Structure of Scientific Revolutions*
Georges Lefebvre's *The Coming of the French Revolution*
John Locke's *Two Treatises of Government*
Niccolò Machiavelli's *The Prince*
Thomas Robert Malthus's *An Essay on the Principle of Population*
Mahmood Mamdani's *Citizen and Subject: Contemporary Africa And The Legacy Of Late Colonialism*
Karl Marx's *Capital*
Stanley Milgram's *Obedience to Authority*
John Stuart Mill's *On Liberty*
Thomas Paine's *Common Sense*
Thomas Paine's *Rights of Man*
Geoffrey Parker's *Global Crisis: War, Climate Change and Catastrophe in the Seventeenth Century*
Jonathan Riley-Smith's *The First Crusade and the Idea of Crusading*
Jean-Jacques Rousseau's *The Social Contract*
Joan Wallach Scott's *Gender and the Politics of History*
Theda Skocpol's *States and Social Revolutions*
Adam Smith's *The Wealth of Nations*
Timothy Snyder's *Bloodlands: Europe Between Hitler and Stalin*
Sun Tzu's *The Art of War*
Keith Thomas's *Religion and the Decline of Magic*
Thucydides's *The History of the Peloponnesian War*
Frederick Jackson Turner's *The Significance of the Frontier in American History*
Odd Arne Westad's *The Global Cold War: Third World Interventions And The Making Of Our Times*

LITERATURE

Chinua Achebe's *An Image of Africa: Racism in Conrad's Heart of Darkness*
Roland Barthes's *Mythologies*
Homi K. Bhabha's *The Location of Culture*
Judith Butler's *Gender Trouble*
Simone De Beauvoir's *The Second Sex*
Ferdinand De Saussure's *Course in General Linguistics*
T. S. Eliot's *The Sacred Wood: Essays on Poetry and Criticism*
Zora Neale Huston's *Characteristics of Negro Expression*
Toni Morrison's *Playing in the Dark: Whiteness in the American Literary Imagination*
Edward Said's *Orientalism*
Gayatri Chakravorty Spivak's *Can the Subaltern Speak?*
Mary Wollstonecraft's *A Vindication of the Rights of Women*
Virginia Woolf's *A Room of One's Own*

PHILOSOPHY

Elizabeth Anscombe's *Modern Moral Philosophy*
Hannah Arendt's *The Human Condition*
Aristotle's *Metaphysics*
Aristotle's *Nicomachean Ethics*
Edmund Gettier's *Is Justified True Belief Knowledge?*
Georg Wilhelm Friedrich Hegel's *Phenomenology of Spirit*
David Hume's *Dialogues Concerning Natural Religion*
David Hume's *The Enquiry for Human Understanding*
Immanuel Kant's *Religion within the Boundaries of Mere Reason*
Immanuel Kant's *Critique of Pure Reason*
Søren Kierkegaard's *The Sickness Unto Death*
Søren Kierkegaard's *Fear and Trembling*
C. S. Lewis's *The Abolition of Man*
Alasdair MacIntyre's *After Virtue*
Marcus Aurelius's *Meditations*
Friedrich Nietzsche's *On the Genealogy of Morality*
Friedrich Nietzsche's *Beyond Good and Evil*
Plato's *Republic*
Plato's *Symposium*
Jean-Jacques Rousseau's *The Social Contract*
Gilbert Ryle's *The Concept of Mind*
Baruch Spinoza's *Ethics*
Sun Tzu's *The Art of War*
Ludwig Wittgenstein's *Philosophical Investigations*

POLITICS

Benedict Anderson's *Imagined Communities*
Aristotle's *Politics*
Bernard Bailyn's *The Ideological Origins of the American Revolution*
Edmund Burke's *Reflections on the Revolution in France*
John C. Calhoun's *A Disquisition on Government*
Ha-Joon Chang's *Kicking Away the Ladder*
Hamid Dabashi's *Iran: A People Interrupted*
Hamid Dabashi's *Theology of Discontent: The Ideological Foundation of the Islamic Revolution in Iran*
Robert Dahl's *Democracy and its Critics*
Robert Dahl's *Who Governs?*
David Brion Davis's *The Problem of Slavery in the Age of Revolution*

Alexis De Tocqueville's *Democracy in America*
James Ferguson's *The Anti-Politics Machine*
Frank Dikotter's *Mao's Great Famine*
Sheila Fitzpatrick's *Everyday Stalinism*
Eric Foner's *Reconstruction: America's Unfinished Revolution, 1863-1877*
Milton Friedman's *Capitalism and Freedom*
Francis Fukuyama's *The End of History and the Last Man*
John Lewis Gaddis's *We Now Know: Rethinking Cold War History*
Ernest Gellner's *Nations and Nationalism*
David Graeber's *Debt: the First 5000 Years*
Antonio Gramsci's *The Prison Notebooks*
Alexander Hamilton, John Jay & James Madison's *The Federalist Papers*
Friedrich Hayek's *The Road to Serfdom*
Christopher Hill's *The World Turned Upside Down*
Thomas Hobbes's *Leviathan*
John A. Hobson's *Imperialism: A Study*
Samuel P. Huntington's *The Clash of Civilizations and the Remaking of World Order*
Tony Judt's *Postwar: A History of Europe Since 1945*
David C. Kang's *China Rising: Peace, Power and Order in East Asia*
Paul Kennedy's *The Rise and Fall of Great Powers*
Robert Keohane's *After Hegemony*
Martin Luther King Jr.'s *Why We Can't Wait*
Henry Kissinger's *World Order: Reflections on the Character of Nations and the Course of History*
John Locke's *Two Treatises of Government*
Niccolò Machiavelli's *The Prince*
Thomas Robert Malthus's *An Essay on the Principle of Population*
Mahmood Mamdani's *Citizen and Subject: Contemporary Africa And The Legacy Of Late Colonialism*
Karl Marx's *Capital*
John Stuart Mill's *On Liberty*
John Stuart Mill's *Utilitarianism*
Hans Morgenthau's *Politics Among Nations*
Thomas Paine's *Common Sense*
Thomas Paine's *Rights of Man*
Thomas Piketty's *Capital in the Twenty-First Century*
Robert D. Putman's *Bowling Alone*
John Rawls's *Theory of Justice*
Jean-Jacques Rousseau's *The Social Contract*
Theda Skocpol's *States and Social Revolutions*
Adam Smith's *The Wealth of Nations*
Sun Tzu's *The Art of War*
Henry David Thoreau's *Civil Disobedience*
Thucydides's *The History of the Peloponnesian War*
Kenneth Waltz's *Theory of International Politics*
Max Weber's *Politics as a Vocation*
Odd Arne Westad's *The Global Cold War: Third World Interventions And The Making Of Our Times*

POSTCOLONIAL STUDIES

Roland Barthes's *Mythologies*
Frantz Fanon's *Black Skin, White Masks*
Homi K. Bhabha's *The Location of Culture*
Gustavo Gutiérrez's *A Theology of Liberation*
Edward Said's *Orientalism*
Gayatri Chakravorty Spivak's *Can the Subaltern Speak?*

PSYCHOLOGY

Gordon Allport's *The Nature of Prejudice*
Alan Baddeley & Graham Hitch's *Aggression: A Social Learning Analysis*
Albert Bandura's *Aggression: A Social Learning Analysis*
Leon Festinger's *A Theory of Cognitive Dissonance*
Sigmund Freud's *The Interpretation of Dreams*
Betty Friedan's *The Feminine Mystique*
Michael R. Gottfredson & Travis Hirschi's *A General Theory of Crime*
Eric Hoffer's *The True Believer: Thoughts on the Nature of Mass Movements*
William James's *Principles of Psychology*
Elizabeth Loftus's *Eyewitness Testimony*
A. H. Maslow's *A Theory of Human Motivation*
Stanley Milgram's *Obedience to Authority*
Steven Pinker's *The Better Angels of Our Nature*
Oliver Sacks's *The Man Who Mistook His Wife For a Hat*
Richard Thaler & Cass Sunstein's *Nudge: Improving Decisions About Health, Wealth and Happiness*
Amos Tversky's *Judgment under Uncertainty: Heuristics and Biases*
Philip Zimbardo's *The Lucifer Effect*

SCIENCE

Rachel Carson's *Silent Spring*
William Cronon's *Nature's Metropolis: Chicago And The Great West*
Alfred W. Crosby's *The Columbian Exchange*
Charles Darwin's *On the Origin of Species*
Richard Dawkin's *The Selfish Gene*
Thomas Kuhn's *The Structure of Scientific Revolutions*
Geoffrey Parker's *Global Crisis: War, Climate Change and Catastrophe in the Seventeenth Century*
Mathis Wackernagel & William Rees's *Our Ecological Footprint*

SOCIOLOGY

Michelle Alexander's *The New Jim Crow: Mass Incarceration in the Age of Colorblindness*
Gordon Allport's *The Nature of Prejudice*
Albert Bandura's *Aggression: A Social Learning Analysis*
Hanna Batatu's *The Old Social Classes And The Revolutionary Movements Of Iraq*
Ha-Joon Chang's *Kicking Away the Ladder*
W. E. B. Du Bois's *The Souls of Black Folk*
Émile Durkheim's *On Suicide*
Frantz Fanon's *Black Skin, White Masks*
Frantz Fanon's *The Wretched of the Earth*
Eric Foner's *Reconstruction: America's Unfinished Revolution, 1863-1877*
Eugene Genovese's *Roll, Jordan, Roll: The World the Slaves Made*
Jack Goldstone's *Revolution and Rebellion in the Early Modern World*
Antonio Gramsci's *The Prison Notebooks*
Richard Herrnstein & Charles A Murray's *The Bell Curve: Intelligence and Class Structure in American Life*
Eric Hoffer's *The True Believer: Thoughts on the Nature of Mass Movements*
Jane Jacobs's *The Death and Life of Great American Cities*
Robert Lucas's *Why Doesn't Capital Flow from Rich to Poor Countries?*
Jay Macleod's *Ain't No Makin' It: Aspirations and Attainment in a Low Income Neighborhood*
Elaine May's *Homeward Bound: American Families in the Cold War Era*
Douglas McGregor's *The Human Side of Enterprise*
C. Wright Mills's *The Sociological Imagination*

Thomas Piketty's *Capital in the Twenty-First Century*
Robert D. Putman's *Bowling Alone*
David Riesman's *The Lonely Crowd: A Study of the Changing American Character*
Edward Said's *Orientalism*
Joan Wallach Scott's *Gender and the Politics of History*
Theda Skocpol's *States and Social Revolutions*
Max Weber's *The Protestant Ethic and the Spirit of Capitalism*

THEOLOGY

Augustine's *Confessions*
Benedict's *Rule of St Benedict*
Gustavo Gutiérrez's *A Theology of Liberation*
Carole Hillenbrand's *The Crusades: Islamic Perspectives*
David Hume's *Dialogues Concerning Natural Religion*
Immanuel Kant's *Religion within the Boundaries of Mere Reason*
Ernst Kantorowicz's *The King's Two Bodies: A Study in Medieval Political Theology*
Søren Kierkegaard's *The Sickness Unto Death*
C. S. Lewis's *The Abolition of Man*
Saba Mahmood's *The Politics of Piety: The Islamic Revival and the Feminist Subject*
Baruch Spinoza's *Ethics*
Keith Thomas's *Religion and the Decline of Magic*

COMING SOON

Chris Argyris's *The Individual and the Organisation*
Seyla Benhabib's *The Rights of Others*
Walter Benjamin's *The Work Of Art in the Age of Mechanical Reproduction*
John Berger's *Ways of Seeing*
Pierre Bourdieu's *Outline of a Theory of Practice*
Mary Douglas's *Purity and Danger*
Roland Dworkin's *Taking Rights Seriously*
James G. March's *Exploration and Exploitation in Organisational Learning*
Ikujiro Nonaka's *A Dynamic Theory of Organizational Knowledge Creation*
Griselda Pollock's *Vision and Difference*
Amartya Sen's *Inequality Re-Examined*
Susan Sontag's *On Photography*
Yasser Tabbaa's *The Transformation of Islamic Art*
Ludwig von Mises's *Theory of Money and Credit*

Macat Disciplines

Access the greatest ideas and thinkers across entire disciplines, including

AFRICANA STUDIES

Chinua Achebe's *An Image of Africa: Racism in Conrad's Heart of Darkness*

W. E. B. Du Bois's *The Souls of Black Folk*

Zora Neale Hurston's *Characteristics of Negro Expression*

Martin Luther King Jr.'s *Why We Can't Wait*

Toni Morrison's *Playing in the Dark: Whiteness in the American Literary Imagination*

Macat Disciplines

Access the greatest ideas and thinkers across entire disciplines, including

FEMINISM, GENDER AND QUEER STUDIES

Simone De Beauvoir's
The Second Sex

Michel Foucault's
History of Sexuality

Betty Friedan's
The Feminine Mystique

Saba Mahmood's
*The Politics of Piety:
The Islamic Revival and
the Feminist Subject*

Joan Wallach Scott's
*Gender and the
Politics of History*

Mary Wollstonecraft's
*A Vindication of the
Rights of Woman*

Virginia Woolf's
A Room of One's Own

Judith Butler's
Gender Trouble

Macat Disciplines

Access the greatest ideas and thinkers across entire disciplines, including

INEQUALITY

Ha-Joon Chang's, *Kicking Away the Ladder*

David Graeber's, *Debt: The First 5000 Years*

Robert E. Lucas's, *Why Doesn't Capital Flow from Rich To Poor Countries?*

Thomas Piketty's, *Capital in the Twenty-First Century*

Amartya Sen's, *Inequality Re-Examined*

Mahbub Ul Haq's, *Reflections on Human Development*

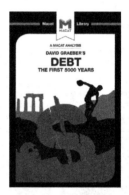

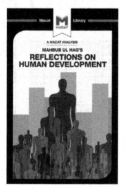

Macat Disciplines

Access the greatest ideas and thinkers across entire disciplines, including

CRIMINOLOGY

Michelle Alexander's
*The New Jim Crow:
Mass Incarceration in the
Age of Colorblindness*

**Michael R. Gottfredson
& Travis Hirschi's**
A General Theory of Crime

Elizabeth Loftus's
Eyewitness Testimony

**Richard Herrnstein
& Charles A. Murray's**
*The Bell Curve: Intelligence and
Class Structure in American Life*

Jay Macleod's
*Ain't No Makin' It:
Aspirations and Attainment in a
Low-Income Neighborhood*

Philip Zimbardo's
The Lucifer Effect

Macat analyses are available from all good bookshops and libraries.

Access hundreds of analyses through one, multimedia tool.
Join free for one month **library.macat.com**

Macat Disciplines

*Access the greatest ideas and thinkers
across entire disciplines, including*

Postcolonial Studies

Roland Barthes's *Mythologies*
Frantz Fanon's *Black Skin, White Masks*
Homi K. Bhabha's *The Location of Culture*
Gustavo Gutiérrez's *A Theology of Liberation*
Edward Said's *Orientalism*
Gayatri Chakravorty Spivak's *Can the Subaltern Speak?*

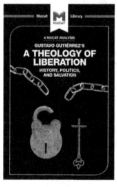

Macat analyses are available from all good bookshops and libraries.

Access hundreds of analyses through one, multimedia tool.
Join free for one month **library.macat.com**

Macat Disciplines

Access the greatest ideas and thinkers across entire disciplines, including

GLOBALIZATION

Arjun Appadurai's, *Modernity at Large: Cultural Dimensions of Globalisation*

James Ferguson's, *The Anti-Politics Machine*

Geert Hofstede's, *Culture's Consequences*

Amartya Sen's, *Development as Freedom*

Macat analyses are available from all good bookshops and libraries.

Access hundreds of analyses through one, multimedia tool.
Join free for one month **library.macat.com**

Macat Pairs

Analyse historical and modern issues from opposite sides of an argument. Pairs include:

HOW TO RUN AN ECONOMY

John Maynard Keynes's
The General Theory OF Employment, Interest and Money

Classical economics suggests that market economies are self-correcting in times of recession or depression, and tend toward full employment and output. But English economist John Maynard Keynes disagrees.

In his ground-breaking 1936 study *The General Theory*, Keynes argues that traditional economics has misunderstood the causes of unemployment. Employment is not determined by the price of labor; it is directly linked to demand. Keynes believes market economies are by nature unstable, and so require government intervention. Spurred on by the social catastrophe of the Great Depression of the 1930s, he sets out to revolutionize the way the world thinks

Milton Friedman's
The Role of Monetary Policy

Friedman's 1968 paper changed the course of economic theory. In just 17 pages, he demolished existing theory and outlined an effective alternate monetary policy designed to secure 'high employment, stable prices and rapid growth.'

Friedman demonstrated that monetary policy plays a vital role in broader economic stability and argued that economists got their monetary policy wrong in the 1950s and 1960s by misunderstanding the relationship between inflation and unemployment. Previous generations of economists had believed that governments could permanently decrease unemployment by permitting inflation—and vice versa. Friedman's most original contribution was to show that this supposed trade-off is an illusion that only works in the short term.

Macat analyses are available from all good bookshops and libraries.

Access hundreds of analyses through one, multimedia tool.
Join free for one month **library.macat.com**

Macat Disciplines

Access the greatest ideas and thinkers across entire disciplines, including

THE FUTURE OF DEMOCRACY

Robert A. Dahl's, *Democracy and Its Critics*
Robert A. Dahl's, *Who Governs?*
Alexis De Toqueville's, *Democracy in America*
Niccolò Machiavelli's, *The Prince*
John Stuart Mill's, *On Liberty*
Robert D. Putnam's, *Bowling Alone*
Jean-Jacques Rousseau's, *The Social Contract*
Henry David Thoreau's, *Civil Disobedience*

Macat Disciplines

Access the greatest ideas and thinkers across entire disciplines, including

TOTALITARIANISM

Sheila Fitzpatrick's, *Everyday Stalinism*
Ian Kershaw's, *The "Hitler Myth"*
Timothy Snyder's, *Bloodlands*

Macat Pairs

Analyse historical and modern issues from opposite sides of an argument. Pairs include:

Printed in the United States
by Baker & Taylor Publisher Services